the
letters
of
Paul

CONVERSATIONS
IN CONTEXT

by Calvin J. Roetzel

JOHN KNOX PRESS
ATLANTA

Library of Congress Cataloging in Publication Data

Roetzel, Calvin J
    The letters of Paul.

    Includes bibliographical references and index.
    1. Bible. N. T. Epistles of Paul—Criticism, interpretation, etc.   2. Paul, Saint, apostle.
I. Title.
BS2650.2.R63   227'.06'6   74-21901
ISBN 0-8042-0208-7

THE LETTERS OF PAUL

*Conversations
in
Context*

In Memory of My Parents

οἱ πτωχοὶ τῶν ἁγίων

Preface

THIS BOOK WAS CONCEIVED in my work with undergraduates. Many of them were trying to read the letters of Paul for the first time and were frankly bewildered. The meaning of these documents was hardly obvious to them, and the identity of Paul's conversation partners was obscure if not hidden altogether. So I wrote this book to assist people like them—those who are systematically reading Paul's letters for the first time as well as those returning to Paul for a fresh look. The book is meant to be read in a few days before turning to the letters themselves and its purpose is to sensitize the student to the background of Paul and his readers as well as to the dynamic nature of the letters themselves. It is hoped that the modern reader will come to know the letters less as repositories of static truth than as lively and sometimes turbulent exchanges over the nature of the gospel.

The book also aims to sharpen the reader's historical imagination in order that he or she can begin the task of interpreting the letters. Any beginning reader will no doubt change his or her interpretations many times (just as I have changed my own); but intelligent reading of the letters will necessitate some kind of interpretation, and I have tried to clear the ground with this book so that the reader may begin. I have attempted to warn the reader against certain pitfalls, throw light on some issues involved in the letters, clarify the backdrop against which Paul's mission unfolds, and show the structure and function of the letter itself in the ancient world.

Necessarily there is much here that will be commonplace to the seasoned Biblical critic, and my debt to the fraternity of Biblical scholars is obvious. I acknowledge it with gratitude. My intent has been to make the fruits of the labors of these dedicated and able Pauline scholars available to the nonspecialist and to help those who are discovering (or rediscovering) Paul to appreciate the need for still further interpretation.

Although space prohibits my naming all the persons who had a hand in this effort, special mention must be made of Professor Lloyd Gaston, who read various stages of the manuscript and offered encouragement as well as valuable suggestions, Mrs. Carolyn Carlson, my secretary, whose diligent and patient labors helped in innumerable ways, and the members of my Paul seminars at Macalester College (St. Paul, Minn.) and White Bear Lake

Presbyterian Church, who made many useful comments on the content and style of the work. Without the help of these and others I am certain this book would never have been finished.

Easter 1974
Cookson, Oklahoma

Contents

Introduction: Contrary Impressions

FEW WHO KNOW HIM are neutral about Paul. Some love him; others hate him. And so it has always been. Within his own churches he was worshiped by some and maligned by others, called courageous and scoffed at as a coward, viewed as true and dismissed as an impostor. In some quarters he was unwanted; in others warmly welcomed. In the second century, Polycarp revered him as "blessed and glorious"; a Jewish-Christian sect rebuffed him as the Devil incarnate. And so to this day Paul continues to provoke and excite, to challenge and antagonize.

A college coed, for example, feels insulted by Paul's view of woman. She is offended by the popular legend which calls Paul's "thorn in the flesh" a woman, and she is disgusted by the command in 1 Timothy 2:12 that no woman is "to teach or to have authority over men." Rather, as it says there, they are to be silent and submissive, earning their salvation by bearing children (2:11–15). How revolting, she says, that Paul should advise male believers, "It is well for a man not to touch a woman" (1 Cor. 7:1), or that he should think it shameful for women to speak in church gatherings (1 Cor. 14:35). Instead, he advised them to bring their queries to their husbands in private (14:35). Why, she asks, should girls grow up thinking there is something dirty or inferior about being female? Why doesn't Paul command the women not to touch a man? Why must he assume that subordination of women to men is an essential part of the divine order (1 Cor. 11:3)? In order to realize her full humanity, must a woman feel she is defying the creator himself? Are full humanity for the woman and Christianity mutually exclusive?

Another student of Paul, however, argues that Paul was no male chauvinist, but a women's liberationist. Paul, in his view, has suffered the double misfortune of being misunderstood and having a bad press. At the risk of sounding defensive, he asks, "What has 1 Timothy to do with the view of Paul?" On this issue scholars are in near total agreement—Paul did not write 1 Timothy (or 2 Timothy or Titus). In the popular mind, however, the viewpoint expressed in 1 Timothy continues to color the interpretation of the genuine letters. Such a passage as 1 Corinthians 14:33b–36 is not, it has correctly been noted, Paul's work. It was added later by another hand to make

1

Paul's view conform to that expressed in 1 Timothy. Scholars point out that the verses clearly interrupt Paul's discussion of prophecy. Moreover, the imposition of silence on women in church in this passage flatly contradicts 1 Corinthians 11:5ff. There Paul takes for granted the active, verbal participation of women in the service. Even 1 Corinthians 7:1 ("It is well for a man not to touch a woman") has its positive side. Paul prefers celibacy not because women are "dirty" or because sex is evil but because he feels that the special urgency of the times requires emergency measures. With the end in sight, he feels Christians should brace themselves for traumatic suffering. In the face of the impending distress (7:26), normal domestic concerns must be suspended.

However, what is overlooked in this chapter is the evenhanded way Paul addresses men *and* women. Concerning marriage Paul says "each man should have his own wife and each woman her own husband." (7:2) Concerning sexual intercourse Paul says, "The husband should give to his wife her conjugal rights, and likewise the wife to her husband." (7:3) Concerning sexual abstinence Paul addresses the husband and wife together. Concerning divorce Paul says, "the wife should not separate from the husband . . . and . . . the husband should not divorce his wife." (7:11) Concerning mixed marriages Paul says, "if any brother has a wife who is an unbeliever, and she consents to live with him, he should not divorce her. If any woman has a husband who is an unbeliever, and he consents to live with her, she should not divorce him." (7:12ff.) So, throughout the passage, Paul argues for mutual responsibility and the equality of man and woman.

The same impartial treatment is given in 1 Corinthians 11. First Corinthians 11:3 is usually translated "the *head* of a woman is her husband." It should read, however, "the *source* of a woman is her husband." Paul is obviously recalling Genesis 2 where woman is made from a rib taken from man's side. Later, God makes woman the source of man (through giving birth) and thus underscores the interdependence of man and woman.

It is Galatians 3:28, however, that best expresses Paul's view: "There is neither Jew nor Greek, there is neither slave nor free, there is neither male nor female; for you are all one in Christ Jesus." Paul felt that "in Christ" believers already shared in God's new community of the end time. In this new age all barriers which divided the human family were removed, and all obstacles to fulfillment were torn down. Although Paul nowhere attacks prevailing customs which assigned women inferior roles in society, he obviously believed they were full partners "in Christ." When one treats women as full and equal citizens in the kingdom of God, it is difficult to hold disparaging views of them.

In response to this, the coed may still harbor doubts. Can she be sure that 1 Corinthians 14:33b–36 was inserted later? Does it really help to say men and women are equal "in Christ" if old patterns of discrimination persist?

And in spite of the short exercise in Biblical interpretation she doesn't like the tone of 1 Corinthians 11:7 where Paul says man is the glory of God but woman is the glory of man. Finally, even if 1 Timothy is not Pauline, it is still in the New Testament and she finds the view of woman expressed in that book unacceptable.

Even in these days of renewed interest in religious studies, many students have a cordial dislike for Paul. In their view, where the teachings of Jesus are clear, simple, and basic, Paul's writings are abstract, abstruse, and complex. Where Jesus speaks of a childlike trust in the father God, Paul constructs a complicated system of belief. The death of a sparrow brings a groan from the God of Jesus; the God Paul knows cares nothing for animals (1 Cor. 9:9–10). Jesus is warm where Paul is harsh; Jesus is patient where Paul is impatient. Jesus is an unassuming, unpretentious—even unlettered— Galilean peasant with a gift of prophetic insight and empathy for the poor and social misfits. Paul, the learned rabbi, on the other hand, is seen as a kind of bully, forcing his dogma on others and merciless in his attacks on opponents. In the view of Paul's critics, this apostle to the gentiles deflected Christianity away from the path, style of life, and teachings of its founder.

Where some see Paul as a corrupter of the religion of Jesus, others see him as the greatest theologian of all time. They point to his brilliant and incisive interpretation of the gospel for the Hellenistic world. It was Paul who took a message that was Hebraic in concept and idiom and adapted it to a non-Jewish setting without dilution or compromise. It was Paul who faced the hard questions—about the gospel vs Jewish Law, the church vs society, Christians vs this world—which had to be answered if the Christian gospel were to remain intact.

Moreover, Paul was a daring and imaginative apostle. As the great pioneer of the gentile mission, he crisscrossed Asia Minor and plunged into Europe. Tireless in his mission and undeterred by hardship or persecution, Paul pressed on and on and on. And he died with his boots on, still longing to go to Spain, the western horizon of the known world.

Where some portray him as a dogmatic grouch, others point to the strains of tenderness in his letters. He tried to be as gentle as a nurse with the Thessalonians. He seemed overwhelmed that a brother in Christ, Epaphroditus, would risk his life to serve him; he thought of his converts as his children, and he rejoiced at the restoration of a disciplined member of the congregation. His pastoral concerns surface time and again. Unquestionably, his gentle admonition can give way to harsh polemic. But was this because Paul was dogmatic and inflexible, or because he felt the essential character of the gospel was being compromised?

Some accuse Paul of male chauvinism, and some think he diverted Christianity from its pure source in the simple religion of Jesus. But many Jews see Paul as the father of anti-Semitism in the West. It was he, they claim, who uprooted the Hebraic heritage from Palestine and turned it into a rival of the synagogue. It was he who lashed out in frustration and anger when the Jews resisted his gospel. It was he who warned that acceptance of circumcision meant damnation. And it was he who as an apostate from Judaism misrepresented the Hebrew religion. Jews find it difficult to understand why Paul the rabbi would call observance of the Law dark and joyless. Had he never read Psalm 19 which speaks of the Law "reviving the soul" and "rejoicing the heart"? Was he ignorant, they ask, of the traditions of the rabbis, which speak of the "*joy* of the commandments"? In their view the acceptance of Paul means the rejection of Judaism. And all too often it has been but a short step from the repudiation of Judaism to the persecution of Jews.

Some Protestants would wince at the suggestion that their theology is anti-Semitic. Nevertheless, many, perhaps most, would feel that Christianity according to Paul is the exact opposite of Judaism. They would question whether all Jews find delight in the Law. At least the story of Richard Rubenstein would seem to suggest otherwise.

Rubenstein grew up as a secular Jew and started keeping the Law in his late teens. He tells of wanting a "cosmic Lawgiver" who would provide order through discipline. But later Rubenstein came to despise this Lawgiver. His hatred of this exacting judge ran so deep he wanted to murder him. Then while mourning the death of his son he suddenly realized that the Law could never give him what he desperately wanted, a triumph over mortality. Finally, while going through psychoanalysis he discovered a kindred spirit in Paul. The release from the Law that Paul found in Christ, Rubenstein found through his psychoanalytical experience. Paul's unshacklement from a troubled conscience in bondage to the Law perfectly described, Rubenstein felt, his own release from deep personal anguish. Thus he came to know Paul as a "spiritual brother." [1]

According to the usual Protestant view, Paul, like Rubenstein, found the Law oppressive. Through Christ Paul learned that salvation has an "in spite of" quality. That is, God loves the individual not *because* of anything he does but in spite of his inability to make himself worthy of love. God simply accepts man as he is. It was Paul's emphasis on this "grace" that was distinctive.

Others get the impression that though Paul differs with Judaism he does not break with it. They note that frequently the traditional juxtapositions of Paul and Judaism have been weak. They observe that Judaism also speaks of salvation by grace. They note that the neat dichotomy between faith and works is not really a judgment against Judaism, for Jewish religion did not make that distinction. Last, and most significant, they find no evidence that Paul ever felt oppressed by the Law. Instead, Paul is viewed as a faithful Jew who came to believe the messiah had come. This belief did not separate him from Judaism but confirmed his place in it. In fine, they feel Paul did not *reject* his Jewish heritage, but *reinterpreted* it in light of his experience of Christ.

So which was Paul—a Semite turned anti-Semitic, a Christian who rejected his Judaism, or a Jewish Christian who saw his life in Christ as a fulfillment, not a rejection, of Judaism?

The impressions registered here are only a small sample of the opinions about Paul one could assemble. Most readers will bring some notion about Paul to their reading of the letters. Even seasoned Biblical critics hardly come to the Epistles with a blank tablet. But the honest critic is always testing preliminary impressions against the evidence, and correcting them if necessary. The aim of this study is to help the novice read the letters in light of their social and cultural background. Through such a reading perhaps new data will be brought to light which may require the alteration or even surrender of our first impressions. Hopefully, such a change will bring our views of Paul into closer conformity with the reality of the man himself.

1. Paul and His World

MOST OF US can empathize with Polycarp who complained that neither he nor anyone like him was "able to follow the wisdom of the blessed and glorious Paul" (Letter to the Philippians, III, 2). Many parts of the letters *are* "hard to understand" (2 Peter 3:16). Nevertheless, more information about Paul and the world of his addressees should make comprehension less difficult. Ultimately, Paul's letters are understandable only in the light of his genius and the gospel he preached. However, Paul's religious and cultural background does help to illumine the writings. It may not explain them entirely, but it does shed light. In the discussion below we shall look at some of the ways Paul's background influenced his message and on the other side, how the background of his readers affected their response.

1. THE BACKGROUND OF PAUL

Granting that Paul's proclamation was informed by his past, was that past dominated by Greek or Hebraic influence? The evidence allows no easy answer to that question. The language of the letters is Greek, and everywhere in them Paul uses his Greek name, *Paulos,* rather than the Hebrew *Shaul* (Acts 13:9). Long ago Rudolf Bultmann recognized that Paul used a method of disputation called the diatribe which had been popularized by Greek Stoic philosophers.[1] In addition, Paul's letters abound in imagery from the Greek milieu. Note, for example, the allusions in 1 Corinthians 9:26 to racing and wrestling; these fit much more naturally into the Greek than the Hebraic context.[2] Scholars recognize Paul's familiarity with the Greek Old Testament, perhaps even his preference for it.[3] Moreover, the apostle freely adopted the vocabulary of the Hellenistic churches (e.g., Phil. 2:6–11). Some have claimed to see the influence of Hellenistic tradition in Paul's allusion to dying and rising with Christ (Rom. 6:5) and in his references to the Eucharistic tradition.[4] Such cultic identification of a man with a divine figure, they say, is compatible with Greek but not Jewish piety which insists that the distinction between God and man be maintained. Even if one discounts any Hellenistic influence on Paul's understanding of sacraments, other evidence reveals his awareness of the Hellenistic world, and his openness to it. This is hardly surprising: some Hellenistic influence should be presupposed if Paul

6

did indeed spend his formative years in Tarsus, a bustling trade center with a sizable and energetic Stoic school. But was the Hellenistic influence dominant? John Knox was so firmly convinced of Paul's Hellenism that he wondered if Paul ever did, as Luke claims, study under Gamaliel in Jerusalem (Acts 22:3).[5]

Yet in spite of his openness to the Hellenistic world, Paul was proud of his Jewish heritage. In Philippians 3:5f. he refers to himself as "circumcised on the eighth day, of the people Israel, of the tribe of Benjamin, a Hebrew born of Hebrews; as to the law a Pharisee . . . as to righteousness under the law blameless." This tradition influenced Paul in a variety of ways. He often appealed to Jewish Scripture. Jeremias has shown that Paul's exegetical method came from the rabbis.[6] His comparison of Adam and Jesus (Rom. 5:12ff.), the lesson he drew from Israel's wilderness experience to instruct the church (1 Cor. 10), his use of some texts to interpret others (2 Cor. 3:6ff.), and his allusions to Jewish legend (e.g., 1 Cor. 11:8) all show how thoroughly Hebrew tradition permeated Paul's thought. Schoeps quite properly states that Paul's argument is obscure if not altogether incomprehensible apart from its relationship to Old Testament materials.[7]

Paul's views on eschatology are deeply rooted in Jewish apocalyptic thought.[8] Such terms as "wrath" (*orgē*), the "day" (*hēmera*), "death" (*thanatos*), "righteousness" (*dikaiosunē*), "judgment" (*krisis*), and the distinction between the two ages (*aeon*) are hardly intelligible apart from their Jewish background. And the similarity between Paul and Jewish apocalyptic goes far beyond the colorful terminology they share. Both are dominated by an eager longing for and an earnest expectation of the messianic kingdom. In both burns that intensity which comes from living on the boundary between two worlds—one dying and the other being born. Both share the link with Israel's past, and both hope for the imminent fruition of God's promises. Although Paul's understanding of Jesus as beginning God's future age differs from the ideas in Jewish apocalyptic, the two share a conviction that this generation is to be the last. This heightened awareness of God's impending doom influences everything Paul says to the churches. Everything he enjoins—instructions concerning marriage (1 Cor. 7:26), or for settling disputes in the church (Rom. 14:10–12), or for celebrating the Eucharist (1 Cor. 11:32)—as well as his own sense of mission, assumes a special urgency because of this belief that time is short.[9]

This combination of Hellenistic and Jewish elements was probably not original with Paul. More likely, it came prepackaged in the Jewish tradition he knew. In the Asia Minor of Paul's youth the Jews had already accommodated themselves to their Greek environment. They attended the theater, took part in sports, gave their children Greek or Latin names, and decorated their tombs with Greek art.[10] This accommodation, however, was made without assimilation. The Jews of the Asia Minor of Paul's youth were well integrated into the community. They were good citizens up to a point. But at that point—where the claims of gentile society clashed with the claims of Torah—the Law took precedence.

Judging by the archeological evidence, even in Palestine Judaism had been Hellenized almost as much as in Asia Minor. Goodenough has drawn our attention to numerous Greek inscriptions found in Jerusalem itself.[11] A Greek word, "Sanhedrin," designated the most significant judging body in Palestine, and Greek manuscripts were found among the scrolls from the Qumran sect on the Dead Sea. We see, therefore, to quote Davies, that "the traditional convenient dichotomy between Judaism and Hellenism was largely false. In the fusions of the first century the boundaries between these are now seen to have been very fluid."[12] Using different information, Martin Hengel has come to substantially the same conclusion in his well-documented study, *Judentum und Hellenismus*.[13] Therefore, to attempt to understand Paul exclusively in light of his Hellenistic or his Jewish background is to misunderstand him.[14]

The most formative item in Paul's experience was his meeting with the risen Lord (1 Cor. 9:1; 15:8). Evangelists have frequently called this Paul's conversion, but twenty years ago Johannes Munck argued that by Paul's own description that meeting resembled less a conversion from the revivalist period than an Old Testament prophetic call. Like Jeremiah of old, Paul said that God "had set me apart before I was born," and described himself as "called . . . set apart for the gospel of God which he promised beforehand through his prophets." (Gal. 1:15; Rom. 1:1–2)[15] That Paul viewed himself as a latter-day Jeremiah is unlikely;[16] but it is almost certain that Paul regarded his conversion as a call, like Jeremiah's, and not just a psychological change. In the view of some scholars the Acts account of Paul's Damascus road encounter (Acts 9:1–30; 22:3–21; 26:4–20) does denote a sudden conversion experience. Increasingly, however, others caution us against making the views expressed in Acts normative for understanding Paul.[17] Whereas the term "conversion" suggests a radical break with the past, Paul's Damascus experience produced no such repudiation. Although he did turn from persecuting the church to nurturing it, he consistently linked the church (or its gospel) with God's promises to Israel (e.g., Rom. 9:4–5). His conviction the messiah had come *distinguished* Paul from the Jewish majority, but it did not *divorce* him from Jewish tradition.

Paul's relationship to Christ was central but it was not exhaustive. Any emphasis on his relationship to Christ which excludes consideration of his background, or any stress on the background to the exclusion of his gospel, distorts our view of Paul and the gospel he preached. It is important, therefore, while reading the letters to remember that Paul was many things at once —a Hebrew of the Hebrews, a Pharisee, a Roman citizen, an apostle of Christ, and a missionary to the gentiles. And though these aspects of his life do not all hold equal place in Paul's theology, each of them contributes something. Alertness to the way these forces work on Paul should give us a fuller appreciation of the range, richness, and subtleties of his epistles.

2. THE WORLD OF PAUL'S HEARERS

In Paul's letters we overhear one side of a heated exchange. We are left to guess what Paul's interlocutors are saying and how their questions influence Paul's response. To get the full force of Paul's remarks we need to know what brought them on, but we can only hope to do that by first getting an understanding of his correspondents' world view. It is not enough to know Paul's world; we must also know the world of his hearers.

At least four and perhaps all of Paul's letters were written to churches in the spiritual orbit of Greece.[18] It is likely that gentiles made up a great, if not the greatest, part of Paul's congregations.[19] Some of the gentiles were "god fearers," i.e., people who were sympathetic or even partial to Judaism but not yet proselytes to it. Others had shared fully in the other religious movements of the day (1 Cor. 8:1–13; 10:14–22; 1 Thess. 1:9). But all, regardless of faith, had been affected by the disenchantment which characterized the age.

The causes of this first-century malaise go back to the third century B.C., a period of severe hardship in Greece. Depression, civil war, near collapse of the judicial system, and the demise of the city-state worsened the suffering brought on initially by famine and hunger. Few found it possible to trust in the old gods. Infanticide was common. The great Hellenistic dream of one world free of barbarism and corruption soured. The hope that Rome with its power could deliver the good life evaporated. As the first century approached, interest in science and clear logical thought waned. A universal cynicism undercut respect for governments and for all institutions. In place of earlier Greek fascination with the body and appreciation for beauty and order in the universe, there appeared a devaluation of the world and a repudiation of the body. The Greek word "athlete" (*asketes*) came to mean "ascetic."[20] Communal piety gave way to individualized religion. As Gilbert Murray says,

> This sense of failure, this progressive loss of hope in the world, in sober calculation, and in organized human effort, threw the later Greek back upon his own soul, upon the pursuit of personal holiness, upon emotions, mysteries and revelations, upon the comparative neglect of this transitory and imperfect world for the sake of some dream-world far off, which shall subsist without sin or corruption, the same yesterday, to-day and for ever.[21]

a. *The Mystery Religions.* We know little about the mystery religions in first-century Greece, perhaps because they were so successful in guarding their secrets. What we do know harmonizes well with the spirit of the time. The central concern of the mysteries was for personal salvation through direct apprehension of the deity. This knowledge was less intellectual than mystical, less rational than relational. Through the prescribed rites the participant received more than a vision, he experienced solidarity with the god. Preparation included elaborate cleansing rites (baptisms), and in some of the mysteries sexual union in a cultic setting offered ecstatic union with the god. Through ritual merger with the deity the initiate experienced the state of blessedness: the terror of history was overcome, release from the corruption of this world achieved, and immortality became a present reality.

The dying and rising god at the center of the mystery cult had had his first home in agriculture. In that context the god's life and death had practical issue as the renewal of crops. Now, however, under the influence of mystery religions, the ancient fertility rites changed focus, from the renewal of crops to the renewal of life after death.[22] In the words of Firmicus Maximus we see how the fate of the god became the fate of the initiate:

> Take courage, ye initiates! As the god was saved,
> So too for us comes salvation from suffering.[23]

In the death of the god the initiate dies, in his resurrection the initiate rises to immortal life. "The initiate is 'born again,' 'changed,' 'deified,' and 'enlightened.'"[24]

b. *Stoicism.* The personal agony and social upheaval of the third century B.C. provided the ingredients for the formation of Stoicism. With a shaking of the foundations, questions of theodicy were raised in the sharpest possible way: If they care about the plight of man why do the gods fail to redress the wrongs inflicted by this hostile world? Why is life unjust and unfair if providence favors justice and fair play? The Stoics answered by affirming rather than denying the divine presence in the world. "God" for the Stoics was less a divine personality who actively engaged in the affairs of men than a divine principle (*logos* or reason) which pervaded and governed the universe. The world itself, like man, had a soul which directed its affairs, and existence was seen as fundamentally rational. Even natural disasters such as floods, earthquakes, or famine advanced the divine purpose; perhaps they controlled population or served purposes hidden from men. Chrysippus once remarked that even the lowly bedbug was an instrument of the divine *logos* because he kept man from sleeping too much or too long. Once a person understood the universe to be fundamentally rational, he could accept whatever happened with equanimity (or *apatheia*). *Apatheia* was not mere resignation (as its English cognate *apathy* would suggest), but a source of strength based on the conviction that all things were controlled and directed by divine reason. *Apatheia,* therefore, was the gateway to true freedom, for the truly disinterested man was untrammeled by the concerns and cares of the world. In the Stoic view a kind of self-sufficiency or spiritual autonomy characterized the life of the truly liberated man.

Although Stoicism was pantheistic (the universe was infused with divine

soul), it was no mystery reli⟨...⟩, however, did
give it a highly individualistic ⟨...⟩ etachment and
the orderliness of the cosmc ⟨...⟩ tory. Since the
world moved in ways prede⟨...⟩ was a certain
sameness about it that mini⟨...⟩ ⟨p⟩ast or a future.
As Bultmann says,

> The Stoic believes that ⟨...⟩ ⟨inv⟩olvement in time.
> By detaching himself f⟨...⟩ ⟨...⟩ from time. The
> essential part of man is ⟨...⟩ ⟨...⟩ss.[25]

Paul's early years were ⟨...⟩ ⟨Sto⟩ic teaching. Although his letters show sig⟨...⟩ ⟨o⟩f the diatribe),[26]
Paul's outlook differs ma⟨...⟩ ⟨con⟩temporaries. His
gospel is fundamentally h⟨...⟩ ⟨histor⟩ical event, based on
a historical person, antici⟨...⟩ (real) future. Unlike the Stoic view of free⟨...⟩ ⟨free⟩dom for Paul means
liberation from hostile p⟨...⟩ ⟨serv⟩ice to Christ. The
Stoic is confident man c⟨...⟩ ⟨own⟩ efforts; Paul sees
freedom as the result of ⟨...⟩ ⟨S⟩toic's concern centers on freedom, and thu⟨...⟩ ⟨s⟩ays Paul, concerns
life, and thus the interaction of men. We see, ⟨...⟩ ⟨t⟩hat while Paul uses
the Stoic idiom he always subordinates it to his gospel. Paul's addressees, however, were inclined to accommodate the gospel to familiar spiritual options.
Such compromises led to sharp retorts between the apostle and his churches.

c. *Neo-Pythagoreanism.* Because of its ability to synthesize diverse traditions, Pythagoreanism [27] enjoyed a widespread revival in the first century
B.C. With the venerated name of Pythagoras to legitimize their teachings, the
Neo-Pythagoreans forged a union of philosophy and religious piety which
had genuine popular appeal. Far from being just an exercise in speculation,
this philosophy concerned itself with cultivating a sensitivity to the divine
element within the self. That "like seeks like" was the primary axiom of both
Pythagorean (6th century B.C.) and Neo-Pythagorean thought (1st century
B.C.). This meant that man's essential nature, being divine, constantly seeks
to return home to its cosmic source; the aim of life is to strip off the body to
allow the spirit to rejoin the divine soul. Naturally this loyalty to one's higher
nature required repudiation of the flesh, because it is by flesh that the spirit is
tethered to this world. This emphasis on liberation from the body often led
to a repression or a sublimation of sex, and a life of poverty free from earth's
trappings. Sometimes a vow of silence was taken to mitigate traffic with this
world and afford fuller contemplation of the world of spirit.

Since the soul was divine, and the divine eternal, the soul was firmly believed to be immortal, and this led to belief in transmigration. But soul was
not the exclusive property of man: the divine element went beyond the human

family to include animals. The Neo-Pythagorean conviction that the divine ether was present in animals led them to ban the eating of meat and to forbid the wearing of clothes made from skins.

A strong mystical current ran through Neo-Pythagoreanism. Like the god-intoxicated worshipers of the mysteries, they called themselves *entheoi* (those in whom God dwells) or even *ekstatikoi* (those possessed or beside themselves with the spirit). This enthusiasm (literally, infusion with God) often manifested itself in miraculous works. In some circles miracles revealed the divinity of the one performing them. In this view, divine men by nature perform divine (i.e., miraculous) deeds.

For some Neo-Pythagoreans, numbers held a fascinating significance. Far from being mere abstract quantitative ciphers, numbers were divine. Apparently this reverence for numbers sprang from the conviction that harmony was the essence of divine nature. The precise rhythm of the cosmos as well as the delicate and perfect balance between good and evil suggested to them the control of a divine principle. Numbers, in their view, did far more than just count or measure; the harmonies they evinced corresponded exactly to the harmonies of the cosmos, and both were forms of the divine principle. For example, the balance between odd and even numbers, between finity and infinity, and between the one and the many was seen as a fundamental reality that manifested itself also in the division between male and female, light and darkness, good and evil, etc.

Given this world view, it is hardly surprising that astrology assumed a prominent place in Neo-Pythagoreanism.[28] Although their interest in astrology and numbers did prompt the Neo-Pythagoreans to an accurate reading of the heavens, their aim was not scientific but religious. The heavenly spheres were more than the expression of divine order, they were also its source. The astral bodies were viewed as divine beings whose will could be known through study of their movements. Knowing that will was important because those bodies were thought to determine the destiny of the world. Human history, therefore, in this view, was governed by a will beyond it, not by the will of men or by any earthbound laws.

In the view of some, Neo-Pythagoreanism was a degenerate philosophy.[29] The movement did address itself, however, to a major concern of the time. Increasingly, men felt ruled by powers they could not understand. Life seemed capricious and unfair; the only certainty was uncertainty. The elder Pliny articulated a widespread feeling in the cities when he said,

> we are so much at the mercy of chance
> that Chance herself, by whom God is
> proved uncertain, takes the place of God.[30]

Added to this sense of helplessness before powerful forces was a growing suspicion that the powers were careless. Men felt as if they were mere play-family to include animals. The Neo-Pythagorean conviction that the divine ether was present in animals led them to ban the eating of meat and to forbid the wearing of clothes made from skins.

A strong mystical current ran through Neo-Pythagoreanism. Like the god-intoxicated worshipers of the mysteries, they called themselves *entheoi* (those in whom God dwells) or even *ekstatikoi* (those possessed or beside themselves with the spirit). This enthusiasm (literally, infusion with God) often manifested itself in miraculous works. In some circles miracles revealed the divinity of the one performing them. In this view, divine men by nature perform divine (i.e., miraculous) deeds.

For some Neo-Pythagoreans, numbers held a fascinating significance. Far from being mere abstract quantitative ciphers, numbers were divine. Apparently this reverence for numbers sprang from the conviction that harmony was the essence of divine nature. The precise rhythm of the cosmos as well as the delicate and perfect balance between good and evil suggested to them the control of a divine principle. Numbers, in their view, did far more than just count or measure; the harmonies they evinced corresponded exactly to the harmonies of the cosmos, and both were forms of the divine principle. For example, the balance between odd and even numbers, between finity and infinity, and between the one and the many was seen as a fundamental reality that manifested itself also in the division between male and female, light and darkness, good and evil, etc.

Given this world view, it is hardly surprising that astrology assumed a prominent place in Neo-Pythagoreanism.[28] Although their interest in astrology and numbers did prompt the Neo-Pythagoreans to an accurate reading of the heavens, their aim was not scientific but religious. The heavenly spheres were more than the expression of divine order, they were also its source. The astral bodies were viewed as divine beings whose will could be known through study of their movements. Knowing that will was important because those bodies were thought to determine the destiny of the world. Human history, therefore, in this view, was governed by a will beyond it, not by the will of men or by any earthbound laws.

In the view of some, Neo-Pythagoreanism was a degenerate philosophy.[29] The movement did address itself, however, to a major concern of the time. Increasingly, men felt ruled by powers they could not understand. Life seemed capricious and unfair; the only certainty was uncertainty. The elder Pliny articulated a widespread feeling in the cities when he said,

> we are so much at the mercy of chance
> that Chance herself, by whom God is
> proved uncertain, takes the place of God.[30]

Added to this sense of helplessness before powerful forces was a growing suspicion that the powers were careless. Men felt as if they were mere play-

soul), it was no mystery religion. Its emphasis on the inner life, however, did give it a highly individualistic character. Its stress on personal detachment and the orderliness of the cosmos undermined any interest in history. Since the world moved in ways predetermined by cosmic reason there was a certain sameness about it that minimized the importance of either a past or a future. As Bultmann says,

> The Stoic believes that it is possible to escape from his involvement in time. By detaching himself from the world he detaches himself from time. The essential part of man is the Logos, and the Logos is timeless.[25]

Paul's early years were spent in Tarsus, a center of Stoic teaching. Although his letters show signs of Stoic influence (e.g., his use of the diatribe),[26] Paul's outlook differs markedly from that of his Stoic contemporaries. His gospel is fundamentally historical; it is rooted in an historical event, based on a historical person, anticipates a fulfillment in the historical (real) future. Unlike the Stoic view of freedom as spiritual autonomy, freedom for Paul means liberation from hostile powers (death, sin, etc.) for service to Christ. The Stoic is confident man can win freedom through his own efforts; Paul sees freedom as the result of action by God. And whereas the Stoic's concern centers on freedom, and thus on the individual, Christianity, says Paul, concerns life, and thus the interaction of men. We see, therefore, that while Paul uses the Stoic idiom he always subordinates it to his gospel. Paul's addressees, however, were inclined to accommodate the gospel to familiar spiritual options. Such compromises led to sharp retorts between the apostle and his churches.

c. *Neo-Pythagoreanism.* Because of its ability to synthesize diverse traditions, Pythagoreanism [27] enjoyed a widespread revival in the first century B.C. With the venerated name of Pythagoras to legitimize their teachings, the Neo-Pythagoreans forged a union of philosophy and religious piety which had genuine popular appeal. Far from being just an exercise in speculation, this philosophy concerned itself with cultivating a sensitivity to the divine element within the self. That "like seeks like" was the primary axiom of both Pythagorean (6th century B.C.) and Neo-Pythagorean thought (1st century B.C.). This meant that man's essential nature, being divine, constantly seeks to return home to its cosmic source; the aim of life is to strip off the body to allow the spirit to rejoin the divine soul. Naturally this loyalty to one's higher nature required repudiation of the flesh, because it is by flesh that the spirit is tethered to this world. This emphasis on liberation from the body often led to a repression or a sublimation of sex, and a life of poverty free from earth's trappings. Sometimes a vow of silence was taken to mitigate traffic with this world and afford fuller contemplation of the world of spirit.

Since the soul was divine, and the divine eternal, the soul was firmly believed to be immortal, and this led to belief in transmigration. But soul was not the exclusive property of man: the divine element went beyond the human

things of Fate (*Moira*), Chance (*Tyche*), or Necessity (*Ananke*). Life, they believed, was determined by forces which were fundamentally irrational, and which were blind to any moral distinctions. Although Neo-Pythagoreanism was not rational and did not encourage reason, it did offer an alternative to surrendering before Fate. It promised man a way out of this world. By touching the divine within himself, man could anticipate liberation of the divine spark from its fleshly prison, and a reunion of it with the source. Freed from the tyranny of capricious, irrational powers, life assumed meaning and purpose, which made it tolerable.

The character of first-century Neo-Pythagorean thought is perhaps best exhibited in Apollonius of Tyana. Although his highly romanticized biography was not commissioned until A.D. 216 (over a century after his death),[31] the piety reflected in it conforms rather well to Apollonius' actual first-century outlook. Renouncing wine, meat, and marriage, Apollonius wandered about barefoot, clad only in "earthwool" (linen—which did not strip animals of their clothing). Through gifts to the poor he rid himself of the burden of wealth, and through a vow of silence which lasted for five years he screened out this world to concentrate on the divine. His travels carried him as far east as India and as far west as Rome. He conferred with sages in Nepal, preached and performed miracles throughout Asia Minor and Greece, visited naked sages on the upper Nile, and advised public officials in Rome.

His preaching emphasized a strong link between salvation and self-knowledge. Inasmuch as knowing the self means knowing the divine within the self, self-knowledge is synonymous with knowing or even becoming god. Consequently, to know oneself is to know all things, since God knows everything. Moreover, the truly good man is the god man, i.e., one whose actions reflect what he essentially is. These divine acts reach beyond high moral concerns to include miraculous deeds. In the biographical account, for example, Apollonius not only denounces Roman tyranny, repudiates gladiatorial combat, exhorts the common people to improve their morals, and admonishes all men to be responsible citizens, but he also predicts a plague, raises a dead girl, heals a boy bitten by a mad dog, exorcises demons, and quells riots. There is little cause for wonder that Apollonius is asked at his trial, "Why do people call you god?" and his answer is not surprising: "Everyman believed to be good is honored with the title god." [32]

Persecuted under Nero for his "meddlesome business," he was apparently martyred under Domitian near the end of the first century. One tradition, however, speaks of an end befitting an immortal, namely his mysterious disappearance and ascension before the date set for his execution.

Although the biography of Apollonius is late, his activity as a wonder worker, wise man, lawgiver, and patron of the mysteries is in tune with the spirit of the age. Whereas the literary portrait of Apollonius painted by Philostratus reflects some later concerns, the basic outline of his sketch closely resembles the picture of first-century Neo-Pythagoreanism presented by others.[33] Given the spiritual vacuum and the fatalistic outlook of the period and given the hopeful emphases of Neo-Pythagoreanism, its success among rich and poor, privileged and slave, intellectuals and illiterate, is hardly surprising. And considering its broad popular appeal, the likelihood is great it influenced some of Paul's hearers, perhaps rather significantly.

d. *Gnosticism.* Gnosticism (from the Greek word *gnosis* meaning knowledge) was an important element in the experience of the early church. Whether Gnosticism antedated Christianity is much debated, but Gnostic materials with sources which go back to the second century of the Christian era were discovered at Nag Hammadi in southern Egypt in 1945. These materials, now being published, should assist us in sketching with some precision the contours of thought in this philosophy. The description of Gnosticism given by the church fathers was formerly discounted because of its polemical nature. Already we have learned from the Nag Hammadi materials that the picture of Gnosticism drawn by the fathers was not the caricature we had suspected. Since our earliest knowledge is of second-century Gnosticism, it is not always applicable to Paul, but certain features of the second-century version were undoubtedly present in the first.

The presence of the divine *logos* in the natural world allowed the Stoic to view his environment positively. The Gnostic, however, saw his world as incurably evil. It was assumed, therefore, that its creator must also be evil. Yahweh, the god of this evil world, was called an anti-god or demonic god opposed to the true, high god. This radical dualism between the god above and the god below, between matter and spirit, between light and darkness, between knowledge and ignorance, formed the nucleus of Gnostic thought. And the denigration of matter profoundly influenced the Gnostic view of man. The product of an evil conspiracy, imprisoned in a demonic world, unconscious of the divine spark within him, man wanders aimlessly in perpetual stupor. Were it not for the great high god who takes pity on man and sends a redeemer to remind him of his true destiny, man would be hopelessly lost. But once awakened from the ignorance of his divine origin, man enjoys total salvation here and now. Liberated from the bodily prison the "spiritual" man already knows absolute freedom, a freedom which embraces both stringent asceticism and voluptuary license. In his repudiation of the flesh (asceticism) the Gnostic demonstrated his freedom *over* the body. In his indulgence of the flesh (promiscuity) the Gnostic demonstrated his freedom *from* the body, in that what is done in the body does not affect the real self. Although it is unlikely that Gnosticism was merely an acute Hellenization of Christianity, as Harnack claimed, it surely was at home in the Hellenistic context.

e. *Judaism.* Given the presence of Jews in all the major cities of the Mediterranean world (Acts 15:21), we must assume some Jewish influence on Paul's hearers. Baron's estimate that every tenth Roman was a Jew and that twenty percent of the population of the Empire east of Italy was Jewish sounds incredibly high;[34] nevertheless, it is widely granted that the Jewish minority exercised an influence on the Hellenistic world out of all proportion to its size.

Paul, for example, can assume that his predominantly gentile congregation knew Jewish Scripture. It is unlikely that this familiarity with Scripture is grounded in Paul's preaching alone. What archaeological evidence we have suggests that every major city in the Mediterranean world had at least one synagogue. We know of nine synagogues in Rome, and that the largest building in first-century Sardis was the synagogue. The synagogue in Corinth was strategically located near the heart of the city. The number, size, and location of these buildings show that the Jewish presence could not be ignored. Moreover, although many "god fearing" men (*sebomenoi*) did not convert to Judaism, they attended the synagogue and were strongly attracted. It was not unheard of for such a "god fearer" to abstain from eating pork, to keep the Sabbath, to study Torah, and to have his son circumcised, while still holding back from full conversion.[35]

Through active, but not necessarily organized, proselytizing, Jews influenced, if they did not convert, their gentile neighbors. Baron could be right that Jews wandered from city to city contending for the loyalty of their hearers.[36] Matthew seems to be alluding to this practice in his condemnation of Pharisees who "traverse sea and land to make a single proselyte." (23:15) And considering the vast commerce of the Mediterranean, recognition of the Torah was undoubtedly spread by Jewish merchants.

Alexandria, especially, contained a sizable Jewish population. Mommsen commented that Alexandria was "almost as much a city of the Jews as of the Greeks,"[37] and Philo, a contemporary of Paul, suggests that the knowledge of the law by "one half of the human race" annoyed the other half.[38] Although Philo's statement applies only to Alexandria, it is notable nonetheless, for it shows that the flow of influence from the Hellenistic to the Jewish worlds was not all one way.

Each of the movements above is in some ways peculiarly its own and in other ways fully representative of the spirit of the age. And apart from these movements, what had previously been central to Hellenism continued— namely, an openness to other cultures and a broad tolerance and even adoption of views from every quarter. Although such cross-fertilization could be and often was fruitful, the risk was great that the new gods and foreign ways would radically alter or even supplant traditional religious views.

One other motif survived—a sense of community or *sympatheia*[39] with the divine. By the first century the heroic period of Hellenism had faded; but if the traditional gods had lost their power to save, they had also lost their enervating characteristics. Men still felt related to a divine principle if not to a divine personality. It was this divine element in all men that bound them together as brothers, erasing artificial distinctions between man and woman, barbarian and Greek, slave and free. Moreover, it was the godly ether shared by the animals that linked man with them through *sympatheia*.

The most significant development, however, in the Hellenistic period was the emerging split between the celestial and terrestrial worlds. Matter was viewed more and more as an independent principle and the source of all evil, and a terrifying rupture emerged between flesh and spirit, between the world below and the world above. Whether this dualism was homegrown or imported from the East is unclear. What is clear is that it found conditions favorable for growth in Hellenistic soil. Even if many of Paul's readers had never read or listened to the philosophers, their views were strongly influenced by the spirit of the age. Once we realize that Paul's gospel ran counter to this *Zeitgeist* we can begin to locate the points at which Paul's readers would find it difficult to understand or to accept his message. Without question, Paul's gospel was a source of joy and hope to many, but the acceptance of his *kerygma* did not change cherished ideas overnight. Only reluctantly did Paul's converts surrender their view that matter was evil, that salvation was an individual, not a corporate experience, that history was circular, or that God could be apprehended directly without need of historical media like Scripture or apostles. It was over these issues that Paul and his hearers frequently clashed. Once these points of friction are spotted we can begin to see the letters as real conversations over real concerns.

2. The Anatomy of the Letters

ALL CONVERSATIONS have a structure. A "hi" and a "see you later" bracket an exchange between friends. A "hello" and a "goodbye" frame a telephone conversation. A "Dear Jane" and a "Yours sincerely" mark the boundaries of a personal letter. These conventions which we all take for granted provide a framework for conversation, and serve as doorways through which a graceful entry to or exit from the conversational circle is possible. And however habitual this litany of meeting and parting may be, it is a vital part of sharing another's presence.

All conversations do have a structure, but not all structured conversations are letters. A telegram, an announcement, and a letter all come in envelopes and all are instruments of communication between separated persons, yet the difference between them is instantly apparent to even the most casual reader. It is the structure as well as the content that identifies the letter as a letter. It begins, continues, and ends in a predictable way. We were all taught early that an address, date, greeting, body, and conclusion form the skeleton of a letter and that all letters have this same structure, more or less. But the skeleton of the letter receives the flesh and blood that make it unique through the information shared and concerns expressed by the writer. Thus letters, like people, share a common frame and yet each is distinct.

Paul's letters, like our own, have a structure. Fortunately, the discovery of thousands of Greek papyrus letters from ancient times has helped us define more precisely the shape of the letter in Paul's day. Study of those papyri has identified the parts of the ancient letter, as well as the function of each part.[1] We now know that the use of the letter-writing conventions of his time was just as natural (or even unconscious) for Paul as for us. But his use of those conventions was hardly mechanical, for Paul, just as writers do today, altered the traditional epistolary forms to suit his own purposes. And it is the alterations he made that tell us most about Paul's self-understanding, his intentions, and his theology.

However complex such an analysis may sound, each reader will recall how carefully he or she pondered the structure of an important letter. The letter from a boyfriend, for example, may begin "Dear Sue" which in and of itself may seem insignificant. But suppose the previous letter began "Dearest." Then the form of the greeting may raise a host of questions. "Is he losing interest?" "Is there another?" "Is he taking me for granted?" Or, "Is he worried and distracted?" And on and on Sue goes combing the letter, looking for clues in the structure to the writer's deep and true intent. So although the anatomy of the Pauline letter may be unfamiliar to us we are sensitive to the nuances that the structure of letters can carry. Once the letter-writing conventions which Paul used are understood, the alert reader will also find clues to Paul's intent in his creative use of those conventions as well.

The discussion below will treat both the form and the function of main elements in the Pauline letter. Our purpose is to show the working of the separate parts, not to offer an exhaustive discussion of each member. Before turning to our survey of the separate members of the letter, let us display a typical Greek papyrus letter. From such a model the basic skeleton of the letter will become clear, and we shall better understand how Paul duplicates letter-writing patterns of his own time as well as how he alters them.

Irenaeus to Apollinarius his dearest brother many greetings. I pray continually for your health, and I myself am well. I wish you to know that I reached land on the sixth of the month Epeiph and we unloaded our cargo on the eighteenth of the same month. I went up to Rome, on the twenty-fifth of the same month and the place welcomed us as the god willed, and we are daily expecting our discharge, it so being that up till to-day nobody in the corn fleet has been released. Many salutations to your wife and to Serenus and to all who love you, each by name. Goodbye. Mesare 9.[a]	SALUTATION PRAYER BODY CONCLUSION (Greetings, final wish, date)

A comparison of the key elements in this letter with those in Paul's letter to Philemon may be illuminating:

		Papyrus Letter	*Pauline Letter*
I. SALUTATION			
	A. Sender	Irenaeus	Paul, a prisoner for Christ Jesus, and Timothy our brother
	B. Recipient	to Apollinarius his dearest brother	To Philemon our beloved fellow worker and Apphia our sister and Archippus our fellow soldier, and the church in your house
	C. Greeting	many greetings	Grace to you and peace from God our Father and the Lord Jesus Christ

	Papyrus Letter	*Pauline Letter*
II. THANKSGIVING (Prayer)	I pray continually for your health, and I myself am well.	I thank my God always when I remember you in my prayers
III. BODY	(Information about his arrival on the grain boat from Egypt to Rome)	(Discussion of return of Onesimus the slave)
IV. CLOSING COMMANDS	(Missing here but present elsewhere)	receive him . . . charge that to my account . . . Refresh my heart in Christ . . . prepare a guest room for me . . .
V. CONCLUSION A. Peace Wish	(Absent)	(Present elsewhere but absent in Phil.)
B. Greetings	Many salutations to your wife and to Serenus and to all who love you, each by name.	Epaphras, my fellow prisoner in Christ Jesus, sends greetings to you, and so do Mark, Aristarchus, Demas, and Luke, my fellow workers.
C. Kiss	(Absent)	(Absent in Phil. but present elsewhere)
D. Close (Grace Benediction)	Goodbye.	The grace of the Lord Jesus Christ be with your spirit.

Although we can draw no firm conclusions from a comparison of only two letters, the parallels are obvious. Other comparisons would yield similar results. It is evident, however, that Paul's relationship to Christ dictated some change of emphasis. The sender is described as a "prisoner for Christ Jesus" and the close goes beyond "Goodbye" to place both Paul's addressees and himself in the presence of "Jesus Christ." Other similarities and differences will become obvious in our discussion below of the anatomy of the Pauline letter. We shall now take each of the parts in order of appearance.

1. THE SALUTATION

The salutation is one of the most stable elements in the ancient letter. The form is rather precise. Unlike our modern letter, the salutation includes the names of both sender and recipient, as well as a greeting. In spite of the highly stereotyped nature of the letter opening, it remained pliable in the hands of Paul. In Philemon, Romans, and Galatians we will see how Paul molds the salutation to his purposes in the letter as a whole.

In Philemon Paul addresses the master of Onesimus, a runaway slave who has sought refuge with Paul. Through Paul, who was in prison at the time, Onesimus was converted (vs. 10) thus setting the stage for the letter. In his letter Paul reminds Philemon that apostolic mission gave him (Paul) a prior claim on Onesimus. Moreover, while he was in jail he needed the slave's assistance. Nevertheless, Paul reports that he is returning Onesimus with the request that he be treated "like a brother." It is interesting that as early as the salutation Paul identifies himself as "a prisoner for Christ Jesus." Thus the condition central to Paul's plea for leniency to Onesimus (the condition of bondage) surfaces in the opening line of the letter.

It is in Romans that we see Paul's most original adaptation of the conventional letter opening. Writing a church which he has neither founded nor visited, Paul was eager to establish the "orthodoxy" [3] of his gospel and the legitimacy of his apostleship. In some quarters Paul was looked upon as a theological maverick, and an interloper (if not a troublemaker) in the apostolic circle. It is quite likely that Paul's awareness of his notoriety inspired the baroque formulation in Romans 1:1–7. The salutation found there includes both a summary of Paul's gospel and a definition of his apostolic mission. The message which he proclaims, Paul says, is no dangerous innovation but is derived from the promises which God made "through his prophets in the holy scriptures." (1:2) Drawing on traditional formulations, Paul summarizes his gospel for all to judge. He tells of Jesus' descent from David, God's designation of Jesus as "Son of God" through the resurrection, and his own appointment as apostle to the gentiles by the risen Christ (1: 3–6). We see, therefore, how as early as the salutation Paul is defending his apostleship by relating it back to God, and thus establishing his right to be heard. And by showing the integral place of his mission in God's plan of history, Paul puts forward a strong claim upon the support of the Roman church for his mission to Spain.

The salutation in Galatians likewise offers a clue to Paul's purpose in the letter. In 1:1 Paul refers to himself as "an apostle—not from men nor through man, but through Jesus Christ and God the Father, who raised him from the dead." Then, with the formalities of the letter opening out of the way, Paul plunges into his main business. What has been hinted at in the salutation now receives careful and prolonged treatment. In 1:10 Paul begins a vigorous defense of his apostleship that stretches through chapter two. He lashes out at those who seek to discredit his apostleship and who are trying to devalue his gospel. By asserting that his gospel is "not man's gospel," and that he did not "receive it from man" (1:11, 12) Paul seeks to establish his independence of the Jerusalem circle and to defend the authenticity of his message. It is possible, if not likely, that the young Galatian church saw in Peter, James, John, etc., a direct link with the Lord, and as Jewish Christians they practiced circumcision. Paul, on the other hand, had received his gospel secondhand from men, with the result that Jerusalem gospel and practice was often appealed to in opposition to him. So even in the salutation, Paul tries to establish the integrity of his credentials ("not from man") and of his gospel. Once again we see him altering a highly stereotyped form to address the specific needs of his readers.

2. THE THANKSGIVING

While teaching at Yankton, South Dakota, Paul Schubert finished his epochal book, *Form and Function of the Pauline Thanksgivings*.[4] More than any other, this work stimulated an interest in the form and function of the various parts in the letters of Paul. Although Schubert's thesis has been refined, his basic hypothesis has not been refuted: that the thanksgiving is a formal element of most Pauline letters and that it terminates the letter opening, signals the basic intent of the letter, and may serve as an outline of the major topics to be considered.[5]

Coming immediately after the salutation, the thanksgiving appears in all of Paul's letters except Galatians. In each case Paul brings into view the situation of the recipients. In 1 Corinthians 1:4–9, for example, references to the charismatic speech and knowledge of the Corinthian Christians are linked with an allusion to the future "day of our Lord Jesus Christ." A study of 1 Corinthians will show that Paul here "telegraphs" the basic concern of the letter. Scholars have long noted that the Corinthian preoccupation with "wisdom" (1:18–4:21) and charismatic speech (chs. 12–14) sprang from a religious enthusiasm that claimed total salvation in this world. Paul's reference in the thanksgiving to the future "day of our Lord Jesus," therefore, indicates his resolve to adjust the eschatological perspective of his Corinthian converts. For Paul's emphasis on a future "day of the Lord" would qualify the enthusiasm of those who claimed to be already experiencing the "day of the Lord" here and now.

The thanksgiving in 2 Corinthians 1:3–7 functions like that in 1 Corinthians 1:4–9 in that it offers a preview of one major emphasis which is to come in the body of the letter.[6] Paul alludes to the abundance of his sufferings through which he participates in the sufferings of Christ. He then invites his addressees to share also in "our sufferings" so that they may also share in "our comfort." Others have noted the connection of these statements to the situation addressed by the letter as a whole.[7] Against those who seek to validate their claims with visions, mighty works, and other prodigies of the spirit, Paul exalts his imprisonments, beatings, shipwrecks, and other afflictions. What his adversaries take to be the "stench of death" raised by these vicissitudes, however, Paul calls the "aroma of Christ" (2 Cor. 2:14–17). In 2 Corinthians 6:3–10 Paul again defines his ministry (versus that of others) in light of the suffering, persecution, and poverty he has suffered—throughout which the power of God has been manifested. Obviously, he sees his own deprivation as a participation in the sufferings of Christ, and through this he finds comfort and strength for his ministry (see 7:5–12). In 2 Corinthians, therefore, as elsewhere, we see how Paul relates the thanksgiving to the situation of his readers, and how the thanksgiving serves as a peephole through which we see the main of the letter.

An additional word is necessary. James M. Robinson has shown that in his thanksgivings Paul is not mechanically following a fixed epistolary form.[8] Rather, the apostle has grafted onto this traditional epistolary form materials from liturgical tradition. Thus he has created a hybrid form. The thanksgiving in 2 Corinthians 1:3, especially, sounds a liturgical note: "Blessed be the God and Father of our Lord Jesus Christ. . . ." We should be aware that Paul does not slavishly follow precut patterns, but creates his own. Moreover, we should not assume that this was a conscious exercise on Paul's part, any more than our own use and modification of the letter-writing conventions of today is conscious.

3. THE BODY OF THE LETTER

After passing through the thanksgiving the reader enters a vast and varied conversational world. The landscape is as broad as Paul's theological understanding and as diverse as the needs of the churches. But in spite of the range and variety in the body of the letters, there is a pattern that repeatedly occurs. A request or disclosure formula ("I beseech you . . . ," or "I would not have you ignorant . . .") serves as the threshold of the body, while the end is marked by an announcement of Paul's travel plans.[9] Usually these plans include a contemplated visit by the apostle himself. Galatians alone lacks any reference to Paul's travel plans. Robert Funk's explanation of this omission is attractive. In Galatians 4:12–20 Funk sees a substitute for the usual reference to an upcoming apostolic visit. There Paul reflects on his previous visit and wishes that he could return again (but of course he cannot). In the view of Funk

> This is a "travelogue" in a situation where travel . . . is out of the question, i.e., in a situation where Paul cannot add the promise of an oral word to the written word, he recalls the previous oral word and wishes he might renew it.[10]

The function of this travelogue is to reinforce the written word with the promise of an apostolic visit.

Others have noted an autobiographical section, or a report by Paul on his activity, near the beginning of the body in most letters. In Galatians he speaks of his relationship to the Jerusalem church (1:10–2:21). In 2 Corinthians he reports on the hardships he has suffered (1:8–2:12). In Philippians he speaks of his imprisonment (1:12–26), and in 1 Corinthians he recalls his ministry among his addressees (1:10–17). In each case this autobiographical note is fully integrated into his theological argument. The report on his situation is made to impinge directly on the situation of his readers. By reciting the demands made on him as an apostle of Christ, Paul is apprising his hearers that like demands may be made of them.

We see, therefore, that although the topography of the body of the letter is necessarily less predictable than that of the thanksgiving, there are landmarks to guide our journey through it. Since the body embraces the full range and richness of Paul's theological outlook we should expect it to offer difficulties, but we should be prepared also for pleasant surprises.

Finally, it should be noted that functionally the thanksgiving and body of the letter complement each other. In the thanksgiving, using the language of prayer, Paul places himself and his hearers in the presence of God. In the body of the letter Paul interprets the claims made on him and his hearers by God in Christ. As Funk well said,

> The thanksgiving looks back . . . on the effects of grace already experienced . . . the body of the letter calls the readers again into the presence of Christ, that the word of the cross may take effect anew.[11]

4. PARAENESIS (*ethical instruction and exhortation*)

At least three different types of ethical instruction are found in Paul's letters. First there is the cluster of unrelated moral maxims, strung together like beads on a string. Often there is little to hold them together except their similarity of form, or perhaps a catchword carried over from one to another. A good example of this type of material appears in Romans 12:9–13 where Paul says:

> Let love be genuine; hate what is evil, hold fast to what is good; love one another with brotherly affection; outdo one another in showing honor. Never flag in zeal, be aglow with the Spirit, serve the Lord. Rejoice in your hope, be patient in tribulation, be constant in prayer. Contribute to the needs of the saints, practice hospitality.

In this short paragraph thirteen different injunctions are given and at least twelve different topics are mentioned, no one of which has much to do with any other. We shall continue this discussion in the next chapter, but it is necessary here to say that Paul is probably dependent on tradition for this type of material.[12]

Second, scattered throughout Paul's letters we find lists of virtues and vices in which both Jewish and Hellenistic traditions have merged.[13] These lists, like the unrelated injunctions above, have only the most casual relationship to each other. In Galatians 5:19–23 we find such a catalogue:

> Now the works of the flesh are plain: immorality, impurity, licentiousness, idolatry, sorcery, enmity, strife, jealousy, anger, selfishness, dissension, party spirit, envy, drunkenness, carousing, and the like . . . . But the fruit of the Spirit is love, joy, peace, patience, kindness, goodness, faithfulness, gentleness, self-control . . . .

The third type of paraenetic material is a prolonged exhortation or homily on a particular topic.[14] Strongly reminiscent of an oral situation, these materials are highly personal and supportive (e.g., "I became your father" 1 Cor. 4:15). Pastoral in tone, such exhortations appear frequently throughout Paul's letters. The bulk of 1 Corinthians (chs. 5–15) probably belongs to this type of material. Paul there deals one by one with problems brought to him in an oral report by Chloe's people and by a letter from the church. First Thessalonians 4:13–18 and 5:1–11 will illustrate this paraenetic style. Both sections treat topics of concern to Paul's readers—the resurrection of the dead and the unpredictable suddenness of the end. And both close with an exhortation ("Therefore comfort one another with these words" [4:18] and "Therefore encourage one another and build one another up" [5:11]).

For our purposes it is important to distinguish individual paraenetic units from sections of paraenetic material. Individual units (including types 1 and 2) appear haphazardly throughout all of the letters. But the paraenetic section knits together the body of the letter and stretches to the conclusion (Gal., Rom., 1 Thess., and possibly 1 Cor. and Phil.). Although some of this instruction or exhortation has little specific relevance for any particular church, Paul often tailors general ethical traditions to fit particular needs. The general admonitions to refrain from vengeful acts, to do good to outsiders, to obey the leaders, and to build up the church occur with some regularity in the epistles. But these act not as a rulebook for solving every problem; rather, they are examples or illustrations of how the gospel is to take effect. These ethical sections provide practical guidance, but they also convey information, make requests and issue reminders (see 1 Thess. 4–5). Many sources of wisdom feed into this material, and by no means does Paul proclaim it as original; but his weaving of it shows a masterly hand at turning general moral saws to specific and concrete account.

5. CONCLUSION OF THE LETTER

Unlike the opening of the letter, the conclusion has received scant attention. Increasingly, however, scholars have discovered in it important clues to the viewpoint of the letter as a whole.[15] Analysis of the conclusion has isolated its various parts with some precision, and in the light of such analysis we can see the particular use of Paul's endings.

Like the letter opening, the conclusion is a stable element in the epistolary structure. We usually find there a peace wish, greetings, and a benediction (or grace). Occasionally, we see an apostolic pronouncement. And generally, all of this is preceded by a battery of last-minute instructions. Bridging the gap between the instruction cluster and the conclusion is the peace wish. Once Paul crosses this threshold with his readers he has committed himself to parting and he soon brings the conversation to a close.

The peace wish, of course, did not originate with Paul. The *shalom* (peace) greeting of the Semitic letter was familiar to him. Used both in meeting and parting the word expressed a desire for the total well-being (bodily health as well as inner peace) of the person greeted. Reminiscent of the coveted "blessing" of the Old Testament, the *shalom* greeting often went beyond the simple exchange of amenities to a joint affirmation of faith. This peace wish occupied the ultimate position in the conclusion of the Semitic letter. In this regard it corresponded to the "goodbye" (*errōso*) of the Greek letter or to the final wish for the well-being of the recipient (e.g., "you will do me a favor by taking care of your bodily health"). The peace wish for Paul, however, occupies a penultimate position in the conclusion.

In the letter opening Paul usually greets his auditors with a grace—putting both parties in the presence of God (e.g., "Grace to you and peace from God our Father and the Lord Jesus Christ"). In the conclusion, greetings are sandwiched between the peace wish and the grace, and thus, the closing peace wish echoes the opening greeting and brings us full circle: (opening) grace and peace; (closing) peace and grace. Before parting, however, Paul once again places himself and his hearers in the presence of God, and the note of promise sounded in the peace wish extends God's presence beyond this meeting point of the letter and into the future ("live in peace, and the God of love and peace *will be with you*" 2 Cor. 13:11, italics added). So although the peace wish is a part of the closing bracket of the letter, Paul's mind rushes on beyond this ending to the new possibilities which lie ahead.

For Paul, however, the peace wish is more than a priestly benediction. It also gathers unto itself some of the major concerns of the letters. In 1 Thessalonians, for example, Paul addresses a church demoralized and distressed: some members had died before the expected second coming; others had fallen into sloth—evidently they quit work to wait for the end. Perhaps some excuse themselves from "worldly" concerns because of their special charismatic gifts (1 Thess. 4:9). So, in the peace wish of 1 Thessalonians Paul reiterates his major concerns. By declaring that God will preserve the "spirit, and body, and soul" blameless at the end, he reaffirms a future that some had come to doubt and others mistakenly believed was already realized. So once again we see how Paul bends a conventional form to his own theological end.

Occasionally a prayer request ("Brethren, pray for us," 1 Thess. 5:25) stands adjacent to the peace wish. Although it has no exact parallel in the papyrus letters, it may have its counterpart in the assurance of remembrance in the letter opening and in the closing request to keep the writer in mind. The Hellenistic letter often opened with the assurance "I pray for your health" and concluded by asking, in turn, for the recipient's prayerful thoughts. One writer, for example, complaining that he is having difficulty navigating the river past the Antaeopolite nome, requested prayers on his behalf: "Remember the night-festival of Isis at the Serapeum."[16] Likewise at the beginning of 1 Thessalonians Paul includes the hearers in his prayers (1:2); and before closing he asks his addressees to include him in theirs (5:25; see also Rom. 1:9 and 15:30). By such usage, Paul shows himself to be a practicer of that vital reciprocity in life that exists in the community of God. In the opening announcement of his prayer for them and in the closing request of their prayer he demonstrates the corporate rhythm of giving and receiving. Paul and his readers share a world.

Following the peace wish and prayer request the impending separation between Paul and his readers becomes more and more prominent.[17] The closing greeting from Paul and his co-workers and the command to greet one another signal the imminent end of the epistolary meeting. Even where it is not explicitly stated, it is to be assumed that this greeting will be conveyed by the kiss.

This kiss has often been viewed as a prelude to the celebration of the Eucharist. To be sure, Paul's letters were read to the gathered church and it is possible that that reading was followed by celebration of the holy meal, but, judging from the text, there is little evidence for this idea. Rather than as a signal for formal liturgy,[18] the kiss stands as simply the usual form of greeting which Paul harnessed to serve his epistolary interests. The letters were not written to individuals[19] but to congregations. Through the command "greet one another with a holy kiss" Paul is reaffirming the kind of relationship created by Christ between himself and his spiritual family, and also between the "brethren" themselves (1 Thess. 5:26).[20]

The benediction, "the grace of our Lord Jesus Christ be with you," is the most stable of the concluding elements. Appearing in every complete letter, this closing formula varies little. Here again Paul has accommodated an epistolary convention to his Christian perspective (e.g., "The grace *of the Lord Jesus* be with you," 1 Cor. 16:23, italics added). Occasionally, however, a solemn warning or sober adjuration precedes the benediction. The tone of 1 Corinthians 16:22 is especially threatening: "If anyone has no love for the Lord, let him be accursed [*anathema*]." In the other letters similar adjurations appear in the same position (1 Thess. 5:27 and Gal. 6:17). It is improbable that the Corinthian admonition is a eucharistic formula which aims to exclude unworthy or unbaptized persons from the Lord's table.[21] More likely the Corinthian command is a decisive reminder of the central exhortation of the letter. The warning includes those who curse Jesus

(1 Cor. 12:3), those who hurt a brother through arrogant use of their charisma, and those who profane the body of Christ. In this pronouncement Paul addresses the total epistolary situation in which the loveless behavior of some believers threatens to destroy the church.

In Galatians 6:17 we see another apostolic warning: "let no man trouble me; for I bear on my body the marks of Jesus." It is possible that Paul intends to draw an unfavorable comparison between the "good showing in the flesh" (i.e., circumcision) of his addressees and the "marks" of Jesus (scars) which have been inflicted on his body by beatings, shipwreck, etc. Paul apparently understands his own suffering as a reduplication of Jesus'; consequently, to trouble the apostle, the Lord's representative, is to injure the Lord himself.

These adjurations are especially harsh to our modern ears. They sound mean and vindictive. Yet they are understandable in terms of Paul's sense of his mission. Paul felt himself to be like the prophets of old who were commissioned to speak the word of Yahweh—sometimes, of course, the line gets blurred between the prophet's own words and those of his Lord. Paul, believing himself appointed as an apostle of the risen Christ, felt he re-presented Christ to his hearers for judgment and healing; and thus, in his view, the words he spoke had the power and authority of the one who sent him.

Evidently Paul views the letter as an instrument of his apostleship. Thus it assumes an official quality that goes beyond the usual correspondence between friends. The letter, serving as an extension of his apostolic presence, places the community in the Lord's company—with everything such status promises and demands. So, although Paul's letters are highly personal and at times deeply moving, we fail to appreciate their scope and power if we ignore their apostolic character.

To summarize, we have noted the importance of reading Paul's letters *as letters,* and we have seen how Paul constrains to his own use the epistolary conventions of his time. We noticed that Paul's message informs and even transforms his medium. Although the letter was for Paul the only mode of conversation between separated persons, it was more. It was an extension of his apostleship. A reader of the letters who is aware of the subtle interplay between form (medium), content (message), and agent (apostle) will appreciate more fully the subtlety of Paul's gospel and the influence these letters have had on their readers over the centuries.[22]

OUTLINE OF LETTER STRUCTURE

	1 Thessalonians	1 Corinthians	2 Corinthians	Galatians	Philippians	Romans
I. SALUTATION						
A. Sender	1:1a	1:1	1:1a	1:1-2a	1:1	1:1-6
B. Recipient	1:1b	1:2	1:1b	1:2b	1:1	1:7a
C. Greeting	1:1c	1:3	1:2	1:3-5	1:2	1:7b
II. THANKSGIVING	1:2-10 2:13 3:9-10	1:4-9	1:3-7	None!	1:3-11	1:8-17
III. BODY	2:1-3:8 (possibly 3:11-13)	1:10-4:21	1:8-9:14 (letter incomplete) 10:1-13:10 (letter fragment)	1:6-4:31	1:12-2:11 3:1-4:1 4:10-20	1:18-11:36
IV. ETHICAL EXHORTATION AND INSTRUCTIONS	4:1-5:22	5:1-16:12 16:13-18 (closing paraenesis)	13:11a (summary)	5:1-6:10 6:11-15 (letter summary)	2:12-29 4:2-6	12:1-15:13 15:14-32 (travel plans and closing paraenesis)
V. CLOSING						
A. Peace Wish	5:23-24	—	13:11b	6:16	4:7-9	15:33
B. Greetings	—	16:19-20a	13:13	—	4:21-22	16:1-15(?)
C. Kiss	5:26	16:20b	13:12	—	—	16:16(?) (see note 22 above)
Apostolic Command	5:27	16:22	—	6:17	—	—
D. Benediction	5:28	16:23-24	13:14	6:18	4:23	16:20(?)

3. Traditions Behind the Letters

WHY DO WE APPEAL to tradition? Why do we quote famous men, poetry, Scripture, legends, and fairy tales? It is not just to enliven our speech, though it does do that. It is not just to overcome the impoverished nature of our vocabulary, though it also does that. It is not just to amuse, though it even does that. Rather it is because the tradition opens up in us a level of insight or being that we had not known before. Through the shared experience of the ages we are delivered from our trivialized view of man and his world to appreciate more fully the heights and depths of the human spirit. This is the authority tradition carries. For Paul these heights and depths were known through the historic intercourse between God and his people. He appealed often to the traditional deposit stored up through the centuries. Through our study of his use and interpretation of those materials we stand to gain a better appreciation of Paul the man, and the word he speaks to the churches.

From the outset a difficulty faces our investigation of the traditions behind the letters. In Galatians 1:11–12 Paul declares, "the gospel which was preached by me is not man's gospel. For I did not receive it from man, nor was I taught it, but it came through a revelation of Jesus Christ." Elsewhere, however, Paul draws on church tradition, cites the primitive Christian kerygma, repeats liturgical formulas, quotes Christian hymns, prayers and confessions, and uses traditional ethical admonitions. These were all composed by men—so how can the apostle maintain that his gospel did not come from man?

The statement in the Galatian letter does not reveal an inconsistency in Paul's thought so much as the severity of a problem in the Galatian church. Paul's Galatian enemies charged that his reliance on the Jerusalem apostles ("human authority") invalidated his claim to be an apostle of Christ. And this attempt to impugn his apostleship was nothing less than an attempt to discredit his kerygma (the gospel that he preached) and reject it altogether. How, his opponents asked, can an impostor preach an authentic gospel? The Galatians viewed his kerygma as woefully deficient, so they stuffed it out with the observance of "days, months, seasons, and years" (4:10), with circumcision, and with worship ("slavery" in Paul's view) of "elemental spirits" (4:9).

29

Paul scorned this Galatian amalgam, calling it "no gospel at all," and he condemned their doubt of his gospel as a fundamental distrust of the God who gave it. In Galatians 1:11–12 he is not denying that he uses man-made formulas in his preaching; he is saying that his motive—his authority—for that preaching came directly from Christ, and a gospel with that authority must be complete, and sufficient. Once the polemical cast of 1:11–12 is recognized, Paul's claim to be dependent on no man for his kerygma does not contradict his admission elsewhere of dependence on tradition (e.g., 1 Cor. 15:3–4). Moreover, Paul can ascribe to Jesus in person what actually came through the church (1 Cor. 11:23–25). Obviously, he viewed the church as the Lord's agent; and thus, to his mind, what came from the church was also from the Lord. The identification of traditional elements is valuable for understanding Paul. His choice of materials tells us something about his theological emphases, his view of Scripture (though all of his traditional materials are not Scriptural), and possibly also his own background. His use of that material, however, is fully as important as the selection he makes. For in every letter he adapts traditional material to a specific problem or issue. Tradition for Paul was no "thing in itself" whose meaning was transparent. The past required interpretation and application. It is important to realize that these materials were not inert deposits embedded in an archaic past. The tradition was for Paul a dynamic reality coming out of a living past, impinging directly on the present and anticipating the future. In the discussion below we shall list representative traditional materials which Paul incorporated in his letters.

1. THE KERYGMA

C. H. Dodd taught us that the apostle shared with the rest of primitive Christianity a basic outline of doctrine. Although the emphasis of Paul's preaching and his interpretation of the kerygma differed from that of his predecessors, the Jerusalem apostles nevertheless approved his gospel (Gal. 2:2), presumably because on essential matters it coincided with their own. The primitive gospel as defined by Dodd contained six elements:

    a. The arrival of the messianic age as foretold by the prophets.
    b. The inauguration of this age in the ministry, death, and resurrection of Jesus.
    c. The exaltation of Jesus.
    d. The presence of the Holy Spirit in the church as a sign of Christ's "power and glory."
    e. The imminent return of Jesus as the consummation of the messianic age.
    f. The call to repentance coupled with an offer of forgiveness.[1]

Although all of these elements appear nowhere together in the same place, most of them surface somewhere or other in the Pauline letters. The following list shows where some of those elements are found:

a. Prophecy fulfilled .... Romans 1:2
b. Messianic age inaugurated in Jesus who was
   born of the seed of David.................. Romans 1:3
   died according to the Scriptures.............. Galatians 1:4
                                            1 Corinthians 15:3
   was buried .... 1 Corinthians 15:4
   was raised .... 1 Thessalonians 1:10
                                            1 Corinthians 15:4
                                            Romans 1:4; 8:34
c. Who was exalted........................ Romans 8:34
                                            Philippians 2:9
d. Presence of Holy Spirit.................... Romans 8:26ff.
                                            1 Corinthians 12:1ff.
e. Who will come again..................... 1 Thessalonians 1:10
                                            Romans 2:16
f. Call to repent.......................... Romans 10:9.

First Corinthians 15:3–7 is a classic example of primitive tradition which Paul has incorporated to advance his argument:

> For I delivered to you . . . what I also received,
> that *"Christ died for our sins* in accordance with the scriptures,
> that *he was buried,*
> that *he was raised* on the third day in accordance with the scriptures, and
> that *he appeared* to Cephas, then to the twelve." (italics added)

2. EUCHARISTIC AND BAPTISMAL FORMULAS

In his hortatory or instructional materials Paul often alludes to traditions which his addressees knew. The reference to being washed in 1 Corinthians 6:11 is a clear allusion to baptism. A baptismal tradition also appears in Romans 6:4–5 where Paul says, "We were buried therefore with him by baptism into death . . . [and] if we have been united with him in a death like his, we shall certainly be united with him in a resurrection like his." And in 1 Corinthians 11:23–25 Paul directly quotes the Eucharistic liturgy:

> I received from the Lord what I also delivered to you, that the Lord Jesus on the night he was betrayed took bread, and when he had given thanks, he broke it, and said, "This is my body which is for you. Do this in remembrance of me." In the same way also the cup, after supper, saying, "This cup is the new covenant in my blood. Do this, as often as you drink it, in remembrance of me."

3. THE LANGUAGE OF PRAYER

Paul frequently alludes to prayer and in some places bursts into a spontaneous doxology (e.g., Rom. 7:25, "Thanks be to God through Jesus Christ our Lord"). Some of his prayers are simply the outpouring of a full heart, but others have a traditional ring (Gal. 1:5; Phil. 4:20). It is often difficult to distinguish between prayers which Paul creates and those which he takes from tradition. It is possible, however, to recognize fragments of traditional prayers in the epistles. Words like *amen* (Gal. 6:18; 1 Cor. 14:16 and 2 Cor. 1:20), *Maranatha* ("our Lord, come," in 1 Cor. 16:22), and *abba* ("father," in Gal. 4:6; Rom. 8:15) belong to a tradition which antedates Paul.

4. HYMNS

For generations before the time of Jesus hymns of praise had been rising to God from synagogue and temple. It was natural, therefore, that the early Christian church, deriving from Judaism, should be a singing church. While the early hymns of the church were from the Psalms, the church soon created new songs appropriate to its Christian status. Traces of this early hymnody appear in Paul's letters as well as the rest of the New Testament (e.g., Col. 1:15–20; 1 Tim. 3:16; Eph. 5:14). The rhythm, parallelism, clearly defined strophes, poetic expression, and the absence of Pauline vocabulary or ideals establish Philippians 2:6–11 as a pre-Pauline Christian hymn. Even in English translation its hymnic character is obvious:

Pauline Introduction: Have this mind among yourselves,
Which you have in Christ Jesus,

Hymn: I

Who though he was in the form of God,
Did not count equality with God
A thing to be grasped,

II

But emptied himself,
Taking the form of a servant,
Being born in the likeness of men.

III

And being found in human form
He humbled himself
And became obedient unto death.[2]

IV

Therefore God has highly exalted him
And bestowed on him the name
Which is above every name,

V

That at the name of Jesus
Every knee should bow
In heaven, on earth and under the earth,

VI

And every tongue confess,
"Jesus Christ is Lord"[3]
To the glory of God the Father.

5. WORDS OF THE LORD

In 2 Corinthians 5:16 Paul says, "though we once regarded Christ from a human point of view, we regard him thus no longer."[4] Some scholars see this statement as evidence that Paul was personally acquainted with Jesus. If Paul did know Jesus during his ministry, however, it is astonishing that he would barely mention the words and deeds of Jesus. If we had to depend on Paul for information about Jesus' life we would know only that he was "born of woman" (Gal. 4:4), that he was in David's line (Rom. 1:3), and that he died on a cross (Phil. 2:8; 1 Cor. 1:23). We would not know his mother's name, that he had sisters, that he taught in parables, or that his ministry was centered in Galilee. If Paul is silent about the words and deeds because he assumes they are known to his readers, then it is strange that he quotes the Old Testament even when he presupposes that it is familiar to his readers. Moreover, even though Paul often summarizes his own preaching, Jesus' ministry receives little emphasis (1 Cor. 2:1–2).[5] But though Paul expresses little interest in Jesus' ministry or the content of his preaching, he does lay heavy stress on three historical facts: the cross, resurrection, and Jesus' imminent return. These salvific events are anchored in history but they possess a significance which transcends history.

As in the Gospels, the words of Jesus which Paul quotes or to which he alludes assume a transcendent character as sayings of "the Lord." The sayings of Jesus occupy little space in Paul's letters, but they add important weight to his ethical teaching.[6]

a. Quotations from Jesus (emphasis added)

 (1) 1 Corinthians 7:10–11: To the married I give charge, not I but the Lord, that *the wife should not separate from her husband . . . and that the husband should not divorce his wife.* (See Mt. 5:32; 19:9; Mk. 10:11–12; Lk. 16:18)

 (2) 1 Corinthians 9:14: The Lord commanded that *those who proclaim the gospel should get their living by the gospel.* (See Lk. 10:7, the laborer deserves his wages)

 (3) 1 Corinthians 11:23–24: the Lord Jesus . . . said, *"This is my body which is for you. Do this in remembrance of me."* In the same way also the cup, after supper, saying, *"This cup is the new covenant in my blood. Do this, as often as you drink it, in remembrance of me."*

 (4) 1 Thessalonians 4:16–17: The Lord himself will descend from heaven with a cry of command,[7] with

		the archangel's call, and with the sound of the trumpet of God. And the dead in Christ will rise first.

(5) Also 1 Corinthians 14:37: alludes to but does not quote a saying.

b. Echoes of Sayings

(1)	1 Corinthians 4:12:	When reviled we bless, when persecuted we endure.
	Romans 12:14:	Bless those who persecute you; bless and do not curse them.
	Luke 6:28:	Bless those who curse you; pray for those who abuse you.
(2)	1 Thessalonians 5:15:	See that none of you repays evil for evil.
	Romans 12:17:	Repay no one evil for evil.
	Matthew 5:39:	Do not resist one who is evil.
(3)	Romans 13:7:	Pay all of them their dues, taxes to whom taxes are due.
	Matthew 22:15–22:	Then the Pharisees . . . [asked] ". . . Is it lawful to pay taxes to Caesar, or not?" . . . Jesus, aware of their malice, said, "Show me the money for the tax" . . . "Render . . . to Caesar the things that are Caesar's and to God the things that are God's."
(4)	Romans 14:13:	Then let us no more pass judgment on one another, but rather decide never to put a stumbling-block [*skandalon*] or hindrance in the way of a brother.
	Matthew 7:1:	Judge not, that you be not judged.
(5)	Romans 14:14:	Nothing is unclean in itself.
	Mark 7:18–19:	"Do you not see that whatever goes into a man from outside cannot defile him, since it enters not his heart but his stomach, and so passes on?" Thus he declared all foods clean.
(6)	1 Thessalonians 5:2:	The day of the Lord will come like a thief [*kleptēs*] in the night.
	Luke 12:39–40:	If the householder had known at what hour the thief [*kleptēs*] was coming, he would have been awake . . . . You also must be ready; for the Son of man is coming at an hour you do not expect. (See Mt. 24:42–43)
(7)	1 Thessalonians 5:13:	Be at peace among yourselves.
	Mark 9:50:	Be at peace with one another.
(8)	1 Corinthians 13:2:	If I have all faith, so as to remove mountains.
	Matthew 17:20:	If you have faith as a grain of mustard seed, you will say to this mountain, "Move hence . . . ," and it will move.

6. THE PARAENETIC TRADITION

A generation ago Martin Dibelius noticed the traditional nature of Paul's ethical instructions (paraenesis).[8] We know now that the apostle drew on pre-Pauline or even pre-Christian traditions for his moral exhortation. Characterized by a terse, gnomic style, these materials usually fall near the end of Paul's letters (e.g., Gal. 5:13–6:10; 1 Thess. 4:1–5:22; and 2 Cor. 13:11) and possess a certain uniformity in content and vocabulary. Admonitions to do good and to avoid evil, warnings against immorality, exhortations to nonviolence, and encouragement of subjection to leaders, edification of the church, and kindness to outsiders all appear in more than one of Paul's letters. Since these concerns are shared by many early Christian writings (1 Peter, Ignatius, Hebrews, 1 Clement, Barnabas, Hermas, the Didache, and the Pastoral epistles), it appears that the main contours of Paul's paraenetic materials did not originate with himself, but were the common property of early Christianity.

It is generally agreed that Paul borrowed his ethical injunctions, but whether he deployed them appropriate to each addressee is still debated. Until recently, most scholars followed Dibelius who held that the paraenesis was constructed with no particular situation in mind, but as a general guide to everyday affairs. To attribute all of the sins enumerated in the vice lists to particular churches would be a mistake.[9] Recently, however, support for Dibelius' view has softened.[10] If Paul gives other traditional materials like the thanksgiving and conclusion immediate relevance, would he not also mold the paraenetic tradition to each epistolary situation?[11] Furnish has shown how Paul gives specificity even to the more general lists of virtues and vices. The vice list, for example, in 2 Corinthians 12:20–21 deals with divisive behavior (bickering, pettiness, arrogance, etc.), antisocial acts (anger, selfishness, slander, gossip, etc.), and sexual immorality—all of which characterize Corinthian behavior mentioned elsewhere.[12] Therefore, even the general lists have specific applicability when used by Paul.

In 1 Thessalonians 5:16–18 also Paul adapts a general paraenetic tradition to a specific situation. In 5:15 he links the adverb *pantote* ("always") to the general admonition to do good: "*pantote* (always) seek to do good. . . ." The catchword *pantote* likewise enjoins the next command, "rejoice *pantote* (always)"; a synonym of *pantote* follows the third, "pray *adialeiptos* (constantly)"; and a related term enforces the final one, "give thanks *en panti* (in all circumstances)." In the Greek each adverb comes first, and the injunctions form a neat parallel structure:

> *pantote* do good . . .
> *pantote* rejoice,
> *adialeiptos* pray,
> *en panti* give thanks.

The parallel construction, the adverb and prepositional phrase ("in all circumstances," *en panti*) in the emphatic position, and the repetition of the key emphasis—"always . . . always . . . unceasingly . . . in all circumstances"—hammers home Paul's main point, the need for perseverence in these acts of piety. This emphasis on the need for persistence in the life of faith is stressed throughout the letter. In 4:13ff. we learn that death has invaded this inspired community; blinded by disappointment, some want to give up. Misguided enthusiasts quit work to await the Lord only to become a burden for the rest of the church. Both the freeloaders and the disillusioned, the brazen and the timid, receive the same admonition to persevere in the ways which Paul had taught them. For their comfort or discomfort, Paul reminds them that Christ will return to rescue his own whether living or dead. In the meantime, they must persevere in the life of faith and retain hope, for "this is the will of God." (5:18) Over and over again Paul urges the faltering to do "more and more" the ways they know (4:1, 10; 5:11). We see, therefore, how Paul structures traditional paraenetic materials, adding key words at strategic points, to underscore the fundamental point of the letter—the need for steadfast endurance until the end. So, even these materials, as general as they seem, have specific and immediate relevance for the Thessalonian church.

Although Dibelius correctly maintained that the paraenetic sections are not the property of Paul to the same degree as are the sections of sustained theological argument, it is hardly accurate to call the paraenetic materials a "bag of answers to meet recurring problems and questions common to the members of different early Christian communities." [13]

TYPES OF PARAENETIC TRADITION

a. *Wisdom Sayings*

(1) Whatever a man sows, that he will also reap. (Gal. 6:7)
(2) He who sows sparingly will also reap sparingly, and he who sows bountifully will also reap bountifully. (2 Cor. 9:6)
(3) Bad company ruins good morals. (1 Cor. 15:33)
(4) A little leaven leavens the whole lump. (Gal. 5:9)

b. *Vice and Virtue Lists*

(1) They were filled with all manner of wickedness, evil, covetousness, malice. . . . envy, murder, strife, deceit, malignity, . . . gossips, slanderers, haters of God, insolent, haughty, boastful, inventors of evil, disobedient to parents, foolish, faithless, heartless, ruthless (Rom. 1:29–31; see also 5:19–21; 1 Cor. 5:10–11; 6:9–10; 2 Cor. 12:20)
(2) The fruit of the Spirit is love, joy, peace, patience, kindness, goodness, faithfulness, gentleness, self-control. (Gal. 5:22–23; see also Phil. 4:8 which includes prominent Greek philosophical terms like *prosphilēs* ["lovely"], *euphēmos* ["gracious"], *aretē* ["excellence"], and *epainos* ["praiseworthy"])

c. *Imperative Cluster*

Let love be genuine; hate what is evil, hold fast to what is good; love one another with brotherly affection; outdo one another in showing honor. Never flag in zeal, be aglow with the Spirit, serve the Lord. Rejoice in your hope, be patient in tribulation, be constant in prayer. Contribute to the needs of the saints, practice hospitality. (Rom. 12:9–13)

d. *Developed Exhortation* (or Topical Moral Essay)

(See the sustained admonition concerning the mutual responsibility of the strong and weak in Rom. 14:1–15:13; also note 1 Thess. 5:1–11).[14]

In the discussion above we saw how Paul drew on early Christian tradition as well as Jewish and even "pagan" sources. Paul freely used the epistolary conventions of his time and frequently tapped a vast reservoir of Christian and non-Christian paraenesis. The alert reader will spot these and other traditional materials in his reading. Sometimes Paul will identify the nuggets of tradition with phrases like "I delivered what I also received, that . . . ," or "it is written that . . . ," or "this we declare by the word of the Lord, that . . . ." Elsewhere, however, only a break in the context, an interruption in the stream of thought (e.g., Phil. 2:6–11), or an unusual construction of words or sentences will signal his use of sources. In other cases unusual vocabulary or theological statements which sound uncharacteristic of Paul may arouse our suspicion that traditional elements are present. But we must not merely notice that certain materials are borrowed; we must also see to what specific end. Fully as important as *what* is used is *how* it is used in the letter. How, the reader should ask, does Paul use traditional elements to address the specific problems of his readers? How does he relate the traditional elements to the theological arguments of the letter as a whole? Where does his theological outlook require alterations in the understanding of tradition, and what do these changes tell us about the intent of the letter itself? Although these questions are sometimes unanswerable, they are worth asking nevertheless. For through them we gain a heightened awareness of the horizons of Paul's thought. Even our failures may be instructive in teaching us the limits against which we are operating. But more important, by asking questions about Paul's use of tradition, we discover new dimensions of his theology which would otherwise remain hidden to us.

4. The Letters as Conversations

DEALING as they do with such mundane matters as sex, taxes, diet, lawsuits, circumcision, ecstatic speech and intramural squabbles, Paul's letters bear the unmistakable imprint of this world. Among other things, the concreteness of the letters shows how seriously Paul took his readers, and how painstakingly he tried to interpret his gospel for them. Once we realize how the ferment in the churches prescribed the scope if not the content of Paul's writings, then it is obvious why in considering Paul we must treat not simply his thought, but also the situation in the churches. Study of the epistles isolated from their context is like reading the answers at the end of an algebra book without the corresponding problems. Any one of the excellent summaries of Paul's theology would give the reader a grasp of the range and diversity of his thought.[1] In this study, however, we shall focus on the chief issues under debate between the apostle and his congregations, hoping the reader will thereby gain an appreciation of the vigor and ingenuity of Paul in applying his gospel to particular circumstances.

The precise stages of the relationship between Paul and his churches are not easy to reconstruct. In some ways our task is like that of a detective who, with painfully few clues, must reconstruct what happened at the scene of the crime. The reconstruction which follows of the discussions between Paul and his addressees could be debated at great length. It is hoped, however, that even if our interpretation does not point to true north, it nevertheless may point to that magnetic north which, with proper allowances, may still guide us through a rugged and confusing terrain.

THE THESSALONIAN CORRESPONDENCE (*ca.* A.D. 51)

1. PAUL'S PREACHING

After his release from prison in Philippi (1 Thess. 2:2) Paul came to Thessalonica with his co-workers, Timothy and Silvanus. While working at his trade to earn his bread, Paul began preaching "in power and in the Holy Spirit and with full conviction." (1:5) His preaching was well received and enough converts were made to form a church. Proclamation of the gospel was the first stage in Paul's relationship to the Thessalonians.

But what was the nature of that proclamation and what was its content? Although Paul nowhere records a sermon for us, his letters do contain vestiges of his preaching: e.g., "Now I would remind you, brethren, in what terms I preached to you the gospel" (1 Cor. 15:1); "For you know what instructions we gave you through the Lord Jesus" (1 Thess. 4:2), etc. Drawing on allusions to his preaching, we can reconstruct a model of the Pauline sermon on a reduced scale. Although later different problems compelled Paul to give different messages to each church, his initial preaching was approximately the same everywhere. The summary below, therefore, can be assumed to be the first stage in each conversation between Paul and the various churches.

> Yahweh is God of the Jews, and through the Jews came his promises, the commandments, the prophets, and finally the messiah. But Yahweh is not God of the Jews only. In past generations he has never left himself without witness among any people. Through his creation of the world and his gifts of rain and good harvest God has shown his care for all people. But instead of the creator, the gentiles worshiped nature gods and local deities. God has decided to overlook the error and ignorance of the past, and is once more making his appeal to all people, not just the Jews. His promise through Abraham was to all nations. Now in the last days that promise is being realized in Jesus the Christ who was crucified and whom God raised from the dead. Jesus will soon return to judge the world and collect all of his people. He will come from heaven with his angels in flaming fire; he will vindicate God's righteousness and punish those who reject God and his gospel. He will grant mercy and peace to all who believe in him. Those who accept his gospel will now taste the joys of the kingdom of God, and enjoy deliverance from the present evil age. Repent, for the final days are at hand. Turn to God from the worship of idols. Be baptized into Jesus' death and rise up to walk in newness of life through the gift of the Holy Spirit. Be alert, watch and wait for the return of the Son of God.

2. THE REPORT OF TIMOTHY

To avoid the charge that they were religious hucksters peddling gospel for gain, Paul and his companions worked "night and day" to support themselves while preaching at Thessalonica. Occasionally their earnings were supplemented by money sent from the Philippian church (Phil. 4:16). At first, Paul's own example gave his gospel an authentic ring and it enjoyed good success. But among the gentiles Paul met resistance and ultimately left Thessalonica, perhaps involuntarily (1:9ff.; 2:13ff.; perhaps 2:16; and 2:17).

All during his journey south, however, Paul was haunted by thoughts of the troubled church. Jittery over its falling-outs, uncertain whether it would even survive, he felt an almost irresistible urge to return; but, as he says, he was "hindered" from doing so (2:17–3:5). Unable to bear the suspense any longer, he dispatched Timothy to remind the church of his teaching (3:1ff.) and to encourage it. In due time, Timothy rejoined Paul in Corinth, reporting on the problems of the church as well as what was being said about the apostle. He possibly also carried a letter from the congregation to Paul.

In spite of his best efforts, Paul had not escaped the charge that his preaching was for personal gain. His sudden departure confirmed the suspicions of some that he, like the wandering preachers of "pagan" cults, had breezed into town, covered his greed with false pretenses, lined his pockets with money from the church, and then abandoned his converts when he came under fire from the gentile officials (2:14). Because of Paul's success among the god-fearers, certain jealous Jews were also accusing Paul of error and uncleanness (2:3). "Error" because his gospel did not come from God, and "uncleanness" because he taught men to disregard the laws of Torah and thus encouraged libertinism.

Timothy also brought word about tensions within the church itself over the idle, the fainthearted, and the weak (5:14). Preoccupation with the coming world led some to neglect the proper concerns of this world. Some were so engrossed with the things of the spirit that they refused to work. They demanded support from others in the congregation (4:11–12; 5:14, 19–22), and rejected the need for instruction (5:12). Thus, the leisure of some was bought at the cost of added toil for others. Resentments flared up; tensions mounted, and disorder threatened the very existence of the church.[2]

The enthusiasm of some was matched by the disappointment of others. Belief in Christ's immediate return left some unprepared for the death of baptized friends. Inevitably, questions arose: Does the death of brothers and sisters in Christ mean that they were unworthy of seeing the Lord on the day of his return (*parousia*)? Does not the death of some of the faithful raise questions about the salvation of the rest? Is the gospel a fraud? Where is the sign of his coming? (4:13–5:11) With hope flickering, the temptation was strong to revert to the old familiar ways (4:5–8). Immorality, it appears, was taken up again by some. That others might succumb was an ever-present danger.

Nevertheless, except for the parts about the desponding or idle, Timothy's report was positive. Despite the charges against him, a great reservoir of affection for Paul remained (3:6). Despite the crisis of hope in the community, the faith and love of the Thessalonians endured. But the threat of disillusionment was real, and Paul responded with his letter.[3]

3. PAUL'S LETTER TO THE THESSALONIANS

The outline below sketches Paul's response to the Thessalonians. Instead of the harsh polemic seen elsewhere, this letter blossoms with assurance and comfort, gentle admonition and conciliation, encouragement and pastoral care. In one way or another, Paul addresses everyone in the congregation; the idle are admonished to work; those disheartened by the death of baptized friends are given new cause for hope (the dead will precede the living into the eschatological kingdom); those who know the claims of the gospel but who are at the point of giving up are admonished to persevere "more and more" in their life of hope; teachers are urged to use care in teaching, and all are reminded of their need to learn. Some of the teachers have an apprehension of the gospel that contains misunderstanding and disillusionment; but Paul tries to correct the misunderstandings gently and encourage the Thessalonians to persevere in the life of faith and love with hope.

OUTLINE OF PAUL'S LETTER TO THE THESSALONIANS (1 Thessalonians)

1. Address and Salutation 1:1
2. Thanksgiving 1:2–10; 2:13 and 3:9–10
3. Personal Defense
   a. Recall of the Mission (2:1–16)
      (1) Paul's pastoral work 2:1–12
      (2) Response of the believers 2:13–16
   b. The Mission of Timothy (2:17–3:13)
      (1) Paul's desired visit 2:17–20
      (2) Sending of Timothy 3:1–5
      (3) Timothy's return and report 3:6–10
      (4) Prayer 3:11–13
4. Ethical Exhortation and Instruction (Chs. 4–5)
   a. The Ethical Demands of the Gospel (4:1–12)
      (1) Previous instructions 4:1–2
      (2) Sanctification excludes sexual impurity 4:3–8
      (3) Concerning love of the brethren 4:9–10
      (4) Idleness 4:10–12
   b. Concerning the Dead in Christ 4:13–18
   c. Concerning the Season of Christ's Coming 5:1–11
   d. Shotgun Paraenesis (Random Instructions) 5:12–22
5. Closing (Peace Wish, Kiss, Apostolic Command and Benediction) 5:23–28

THE CORINTHIAN CORRESPONDENCE (*ca.* A.D. 52–54)

Paul came to Corinth in "fear and trembling" (1 Cor. 2:3). Perhaps he was afraid that he would receive the same harsh treatment that had cut short his ministry in Thessalonica and Philippi. What he feared might be a ministry of just a few weeks, however, stretched into a year and a half, and the gospel which first took root in the city enjoyed success in the surrounding countryside as well (2 Cor. 1:1). During his relatively long stay in Corinth, Paul received assistance from Aquila and Prisca, Jewish Christian refugees from Rome who risked their necks for him and earned the gratitude of all of the gentile churches (Rom. 16:3–4, see also Acts 18:1–4).

Most of the membership of the Corinthian church was drawn from the ranks of the uneducated poor. Paul puts it graphically when he says,

Not many of you were wise according to worldly standards, not many were powerful, not many were of noble birth; but God chose what is foolish in

> the world to shame the wise, God chose what is weak in the world to shame
> the strong, God chose what is low and despised in the world, even things that
> are not, to bring to nothing things that are. (1 Cor. 1:26–28)

Of these "weak" and "despised" ones no doubt many were slaves (12:13;
7:21ff.) or freedmen who had won their release. Nevertheless, a sprinkling
of leaders from the community did join the church. The Crispus whom Paul
baptized (1 Cor. 1:14) was called a leader of the local synagogue in Acts
18:8; and Erastus, apparently a member of the Corinthian church, was the
city treasurer (Rom. 16:23). In any case, the majority of both the poor and
the privileged were gentiles. They may have attended the synagogue, and
some may even have observed Jewish practices, but they held back from
becoming Jewish proselytes.

From the Corinthian letters we learn that the exchanges between Paul and
that church continued over several years. Although the history of that relationship is complex, we can, nevertheless, reconstruct the principal stages of
it with some certainty. A skeleton outline of that relationship should contain
the following elements:

1. Paul preaches at Corinth (18 months).
2. Paul departs, settling eventually in Ephesus; he writes his first letter to
   Corinthians (Lost; see 1 Cor. 5:9).
3. Corinthians write to Paul (1 Cor. 7:1), and also send oral communication (1 Cor. 1:11 and 16:17).
4. Paul writes his second letter (our 1 Cor.), answering both the oral and
   written communications from Corinth.
5. He dispatches Timothy by land with oral instructions. Timothy returns
   to Ephesus, reporting that his efforts to reclaim the church for Paul
   were unsuccessful.
6. Paul makes a brief "painful" visit to Corinth (2 Cor. 2:1–2), returning
   to Ephesus in humiliation (12:21).
7. Paul writes a harsh letter (letter number 3) "out of much affliction and
   anguish of heart" (2 Cor. 2:3–4, 9; 7:8–12). This letter (possibly 2 Cor.
   10–13) was hand delivered by Titus.
8. Paul travels to Macedonia to meet Titus who brings encouraging news
   about the church.
9. Paul dispatches Titus with his fourth letter (2 Cor. 1:1–6:13; 7:2–
   9:15), a letter of reconciliation.
10. Paul visits Corinth to receive the offering for "the poor" in Jerusalem.

1. PAUL'S PREACHING IN CORINTH

Much as in Thessalonica, Paul's gospel was enthusiastically received in
Corinth. The essence of that gospel was that the deliverance promised by
the prophets had now become available through the death and resurrection
of Jesus. Through faith in Jesus as the Christ and baptism in his name, Paul
asserted, men and women could share in the saving power of his death, and
through the Eucharist believers could enjoy the fare of the world to come.

"Now is the day of salvation" Paul could say (2 Cor. 6:2). The time had arrived when God would pour his Spirit on all flesh (Joel 2:28), when men would see visions (see 2 Cor. 12:1ff.), and speak the language of angels (ecstatic speech, 1 Cor. 13:1; see Is. 28:11). His preaching, as did his letters, doubtless reflected Paul's conviction that his was the last generation of mankind, and his preaching included a call to the community to keep itself in readiness for the end.

While at Corinth Paul evidently spoke in tongues (1 Cor. 14:18) and demonstrated other charismatic gifts ("signs and wonders and mighty works"). In the face of the "impending distress" Paul chose to remain celibate (1 Cor. 7:7, 26). Evidently these examples had profound effect on the congregation for Paul later devoted extensive discussion to both marriage and ecstatic speech.

2. PAUL'S DEPARTURE AND HIS FIRST LETTER

After leaving Corinth, Paul eventually settled in Ephesus for three years (*ca.* A.D. 52–54). Among others, Timothy, Titus, Aquila, and Prisca worked with him there. Apollos also, an Alexandrian Jew, followed Paul in Corinth, enjoyed good success for a time, and ultimately joined him in Ephesus. If the account in Acts is to be believed (18:24–28), the eloquence of Apollos, his agile, imaginative approach to Scripture, his enthusiasm, his skill in debate, and his resourceful personality, endeared him to the Corinthians. It is unnecessary to assume that Apollos' presence in Corinth caused the problems there, but it may have aggravated certain enthusiastic tendencies already in the church.

While at Ephesus, Paul sent a letter, now lost, addressing certain problems in the Corinthian church (1 Cor. 5:9).[4] We are uncertain what those problems were. Perhaps a rumor of excesses had come to Paul. Or the presence of Apollos may have encouraged forms of enthusiasm which were disruptive to congregational life. Under the power of the Holy Spirit Paul probably uttered ecstatic speech (*glossolalia:* literally, speaking in tongues) while at Corinth. Since life in the kingdom of God was understood as life with the Holy Spirit, it is hardly surprising that what was once an *expression* of life in the kingdom became a *condition* for acceptance within the church. Effect was regarded as cause: ecstatic speech was thought to induce salvation, rather than salvation speech. Angel speech, as it was called (see 1 Cor. 13:1), indicated who was in tune with the divine, or, as they put it, who had "knowledge." Those "in the know" felt so secure in Christ and so sure of their power to prevail over this world that they behaved in ways that Paul would have found foolhardy. Since they knew that idols had no real existence, they freely attended pagan celebrations, participated in pagan cultic meals, and ate meat offered to idols. It is possible, if not likely, that this "knowledge" led some to attempt to live above mere accidental distinctions, like sex, since in the kingdom of God by Paul's own admission there is neither male nor female. "Spiritual marriages" would have allowed men and women to live together without sexual intercourse. It is hardly surprising that such well-intentioned practices sometimes encouraged the very thing they wished to avoid (see 1 Cor. 5). If such a life-style emerged from this "knowledge," then we can understand why the gist of the missing first letter was the admonition "not to associate with immoral men" (1 Cor. 5:9).

3. ORAL AND WRITTEN RESPONSES FROM CORINTH

Chloe's people (slaves?) and perhaps others (1 Cor. 16:17) soon arrived in Ephesus from Corinth to report the deteriorating situation in their home church (1 Cor. 1:11). Boasts about exclusive truth and pretentious claims to religious "knowledge" had brought on fiery antagonisms. The church in fact was perilously close to shattering, with each faction devoted to a different leader—Paul, Peter, Apollos, or even Christ. Each faction claimed that only through *its* leader could "knowledge" be gained; and, intoxicated on its own divine secrets, each group thought only of the glorified life and forgot about the cross. Each faction was eager to give full expression to its eschatological gifts, especially speaking in tongues. These powerful signs, they boasted, demonstrated the truth of their wisdom in Christ. Such spiritual elitism fostered contempt of those with other gifts, led some to disdain the unimposing Paul, and jeopardized the very existence of the church (see 1 Cor. 1:10–4:21).

The cliques also disrupted worship (see esp. 11:17–34). Full of eschatological preoccupation, some celebrated the Lord's Supper as if it were the Great Messianic Banquet reserved for the end of time. In their enthusiasm they stuffed themselves, saving nothing for Christian slaves whose arrival was delayed by assigned tasks. Some were gorged and drunken; not a crumb remained for others. Such self-indulgence and indifference to the needs of the brother were direct results of the religious enthusiasm referred to in 1 Corinthians 1:10–4:21.

Chloe's people also reported that one member of the congregation was living openly with his stepmother without any objection from the church leaders (5:1–8; 13). Moreover, some believers had gone before the pagan magistrate to settle disputes with other Christians (6:1–11).

In 1 Corinthians 7:1 Paul shifts his attention to the concerns expressed in the letter from the Corinthians ("now concerning the matters about which you wrote"). Using here as elsewhere the phrase "now concerning . . ." (*peri de*), Paul introduces into discussion each topic that the Corinthians had specified in their letter. Indeed, by noting the appearances of that phrase ("now concerning . . ."), we can reconstruct a rough outline of the Corinthians' letter to Paul (see 7:1, 25; 8:1; 12:1 and 16:1). Our hypothesis of that letter is as follows:

a. *Concerning Marriage*

Given the urgency of the times, we believe married believers should refrain from sexual intercourse and virgins and widows should not consider marriage—all this, so that believers might devote themselves wholly to preparing for the end. Remember how you said "it is well for a man not to touch a woman"? In this we are only following your example. Moreover, you yourself said that in the kingdom of God there is neither male nor female, and the Lord said in the kingdom men and women are not married or given in marriage. Since we are members of the kingdom, should not those of us who are married act as if they were not, and should not believers divorce any unbelieving partners?

b. *Concerning Contact with the World*

You wrote us not to associate with immoral men, but that is impossible; the world is full of immoral men. And how does this square with your preaching? You said that for believers there is no law; all things are lawful. So what is there to fear? Don't we give evidence of our faith by exercising our freedom in Christ? Doesn't God love all men moral and immoral alike?

Also, what harm can come from eating idol meat? Since there is only one God we know that an idol has no real existence. Moreover, we know that physical things cannot defile the spirit—"food is meant for the belly and the belly for food." Must we decline all invitations to eat with our unbelieving friends and relatives? Must we insult them by asking if the meat they offer us is pure? How can we witness to unbelievers if we offend them?

c. *Concerning Worship*

Since all are one in Christ, the distinctions between men and women are artificial; such physical accidents mean nothing in the kingdom of God. It is entirely appropriate, therefore, for women to pray with heads uncovered and to share actively in the service. And why should you have reservations now about speaking in tongues? We are merely following your example. It is clear to us that those who are unable to speak the language of angels have not fully surrendered to God's Spirit.

d. *Concerning the Resurrection*

Through baptism we have already passed from death to the resurrected life. If we have already died, and if today is the day of salvation, how can you say we must prepare for the resurrection of the dead? How can those who have died die again? Also, what do you mean by the "resurrection of the body"? The whole idea of the resuscitation of a dead corpse is repugnant. Salvation brings release from our bodies; what good is salvation if we are still imprisoned in our bodies?

e. *Concerning the Collection*

Although we are poor ourselves, we shall give something for the poor in Jerusalem. It would probably be best if we sent someone from our church to deliver the offering. You would not want anyone to think you were skimming off part of the gift for yourself.

f. *Concerning Apollos*

Could you encourage Apollos to return to Corinth? He had a very effective ministry here. Some of our people miss his powerful witness, and his persuasive teaching of Scripture; and they are always asking when he will return to continue his work among us.

4. PAUL'S WRITTEN REPLY TO THE ORAL REPORT
AND THE LETTER FROM CORINTH

In what we know as 1 Corinthians we see Paul's reply to two communications from Corinth—one oral and one written. It is interesting that Paul responds in kind, sending 1 Corinthians (which was really his second letter) from Ephesus by sea (1 Cor. 5:7–8, *ca.* Easter, A.D. 55) and dispatching Timothy by land (1 Cor. 4:17) with oral instructions. Paul's letter is intact of course, but for the sake of clarity we summarize his argument below.

a. *Paul's Response to the Oral Report*
(1) CONCERNING DIVISION (1:10–4:21)

Why do you boast of your baptism in the name of people like me, Apollos, Peter, and even Christ? Is Christ divided? Were you baptized in the name of Paul? Does some special wisdom come in baptism through your union with Christ? Is that why you call yourselves wise, mature, and spiritual? Your boasting is silly, and contrary to the ways of God himself. His wisdom looks like foolishness to men. Through a cross, or through a motley collection of people like yourselves, or through a frail and unimposing figure like me, he reveals his wisdom—not in strength and glory but in weakness and shame! Christ crucified, not Christ glorified was the heart of my gospel and this Christ forms the foundation of the church. All work laid on that foundation by Apollos or anybody else will be tested on the last day. To those inflated with their own self-esteem and who are heedless of the welfare of the church, let me say: if they destroy the church God will destroy them. Is it because you think you are so spiritual that you presume to judge Christ's apostles, and think you are above Scripture (see 1 Cor. 4:6 *huper ha gegraptai*)? When I come I will find out how really spiritual these people are.

(2) CONCERNING IMMORALITY (5:1–6:11)
(a) *Incest* (5:1–13)

I hear that a man is living with his "father's wife," all in the name of the Lord Jesus, and worse, you condone it! You say Christians are above such trivial differences as those of sex, and that life in the kingdom is trans-sexual. You tolerate behavior which even the pagans scorn. Root out this offender lest he poison the whole congregation. When I wrote that you should not associate with immoral men, I meant just such men as this, not the outsiders.

(b) *Lawsuits* (6:1–11)

I hear that some of you are defrauding others, and that someone has taken his case to the civil courts. Why should you who someday will judge the heathen, or even angels, turn to the heathen for justice? Must the exploited turn to the civil courts? You claim to be wise (*sophos*); are you not wise enough to render a decision on such matters? Great harm can be done to the church and the mission by such action.

(3) CONCERNING THE LORD'S SUPPER (11:17–34)

Each one eats, so I hear, regardless of the needs of others, and only to satisfy himself. You claim to be celebrating your life in the kingdom, but instead you profane the Lord's body. Do you not know that Christ is in his community? Your selfish and greedy behavior not only insults your brother, it offends the Lord himself who is present for judgment. That is why some are sick and some have died.

b. *Paul's Response to the Corinthians' Letter*
(1) CONCERNING MARRIAGE (7:1–40)

I fear you misunderstood my remark that it is better for a man not to touch a woman. Because you think you are equal to angels you claim to be above such worldly things.[6] The pure want to rid themselves of unbelieving partners. Continence within marriage is expected. Widows and virgins are made to feel inferior if they marry. I encouraged all to remain as I am because of the special urgency of the times (the end is near), not because we have overcome the world. Not everyone has the gift of celibacy. It is better to marry than to be aflame with passion.

(2) CONCERNING IDOL MEAT (8:1–11:1)

It is true that there is no God but one, and, therefore, idols have no real existence. Since idols do not exist, you ask, what harm comes from eating meat offered to them? But what if my freedom causes a weaker brother to stumble? Freedom must always be subordinated to love. I am free, am I not? Yet I freely surrender my "rights" for the sake of others. Because you are washed and now eat supernatural food, do not think that you are infallible. Israel too was a sacramental community and yet 23,000 died in a single day in the wilderness. You cannot worship the living God one day and share in pagan worship the next. One is bound to whatever he worships. You can't share the cup of Christ and the cup or food of idols. Remember also that even if you are free in Christ, and even if all things are lawful, not all things are helpful. Eat in a way that strengthens yourself and others.

(3) CONCERNING DISTINCTIONS BETWEEN MEN AND WOMEN (11:2–16)

Some of you say that in Christ there is neither male nor female. It is true that I encouraged women to participate in the service. But you seek to obliterate all distinctions between male and female. Such are accidents of birth, you say, and after sharing in the new creation all such accidental distinctions should be ignored. You claim too much. We are not yet angels. Let men *and* women continue sharing in the service of worship, but let us maintain the distinction between male and female. Men, cut your hair, and women, cover your heads (or wear veils).

(4) CONCERNING SPIRITUAL GIFTS (12–14)

You claim to follow my example in practicing ecstatic speech. You do well to exalt the spiritual gifts, but if those who speak in tongues despise those who do not, how does that build up the church? Strive for the higher gifts like teaching and interpreting which edify others. Allow everyone to contribute in his own way with whatever gift he has, and subordinate all of the gifts to love.

(5) CONCERNING THE RESURRECTION (15:1–58)

Remember the gospel that I preached that Christ died, was buried, and was raised. His raising was the first of the general resurrection soon to be completed. You say you have already been raised up, that death is behind you, that only the life of glory remains, and, therefore, there is no future resurrection for you. I hear also that the whole idea of the resurrection of the body is repulsive to you. Do you not know that God can give us a different body appropriate to that life? But death has not yet been completely conquered; that will come in the future when God puts all of his enemies under his feet, and the last enemy to be destroyed will be death. Then and only then will we be able to say, "Death is swallowed up in victory."

(6) CONCERNING THE COLLECTION (16:1–4)

Have the collection ready when I come. I agree that someone from the congregation should accompany us to deliver the offering.

(7) CONCERNING APOLLOS (16:12)

I urged him to come, but it was not God's will that he come at this time. He will come later.

5. PAUL DISPATCHES TIMOTHY WITH ORAL INSTRUCTIONS AND HIS RETURN

The second letter, going directly by sea, arrived in Corinth ahead of Timothy, who had taken the roundabout land route. When Timothy arrived in Corinth he found the church still shaken by internal disputes and gravely suspicious of Paul. Soon he returned to Ephesus to report the bad news. Neither his presence nor the letter had healed the wounds opened by internal conflict.

To add insult to injury, certain Jewish-Christian missionaries had arrived, bidding for the affection, loyalty and support of the Corinthian church. They claimed to be "servants of Christ" (2 Cor. 11:23) and professed to be apostles (2 Cor. 11:5, 13). They came armed with written testimonials to the success of their preaching elsewhere (2 Cor. 3:1). These "superlative apostles" drew unflattering comparison between their works and those of Paul. They said Paul lacked charisma, that he was an ineffective preacher. He was frail and hypocritical—a bully in his letters but harmless in person (2 Cor. 10:10). When Paul was in Corinth he had refused money, these men alleged, either because he was insecure in his apostolate (2 Cor. 11:7, 9), or because he planned to cream off some of the Jerusalem offering for himself (12:17). For their part, these Jewish-Christian missionaries boasted of their exploits in service of the gospel. By signs and wonders they demonstrated the power of their message; through visions they gained access to heavenly secrets; and for these divine gifts they demanded support from the church and so undermined Paul's efforts to collect an offering for the "poor" in Jerusalem.

6. PAUL'S PAINFUL VISIT TO CORINTH

Upon hearing the bad news, Paul made a brief, "painful" visit to Corinth (2 Cor. 2:1). Once there he was insulted publicly by a Corinthian Christian (2 Cor. 2:5–8; 7:12) and frustrated in his efforts to reclaim the church for his gospel, so he returned to Ephesus in humiliation (2 Cor. 12:21). His disastrous visit played into the hands of his critics. Didn't his swift departure give substance to the charge that he was a coward? His position in the Corinthian church seemed more insecure than ever.

7. PAUL'S THIRD LETTER TO THE CORINTHIANS (2 Cor. 10–13)

In a last-ditch effort, Paul now wrote his third letter "out of much affliction and anguish of heart" (2 Cor. 2:3–4, 9; 7:8–12), and dispatched Titus with it. Paul arranged to meet Titus in Troas to receive his report. Although we cannot be certain that any part of this letter exists, it is commonly suggested that 2 Corinthians 10–13 contains the heart of this severe letter. Certainly the subject matter qualifies as severe. Here we see Pauline sarcasm at its best, and it contrasts rather sharply with Paul's mood in 2 Corinthians 1–9.

8. TITUS DELIVERS LETTER AND RETURNS WITH REPORT

So anxious was Paul about the effect of his "severe" letter that he found it impossible to wait for Titus in Troas. Instead, Paul set out to meet him (2 Cor. 2:12–13), finally linking up in Macedonia, perhaps in Neapolis, the port of Philippi. Titus brought encouraging news. The Corinthians mourned their wrongs; they longed to see Paul (7:6–7). They had reprimanded the troublemakers and restored order. After hearing the good news, Paul sent Titus and two others bearing his fourth letter (8:16–24) which may have comprised 2 Corinthians 1–9.

9. PAUL'S FOURTH LETTER TO THE CORINTHIANS (2 Cor. 1–9)

It seems clear that the crisis had passed. Paul reveals that he had earlier canceled plans to come to Corinth again to spare the church "another painful visit." He seems happy that the adversary has been disciplined and is now restored; he seems both apologetic and pleased by the work of the "severe" letter—sorry that it caused pain, but relieved that it effected a positive change. Now Paul announces his plans to visit Corinth once more to receive the offering for the Jerusalem church.

OUTLINE OF 1 CORINTHIANS (Paul's Second Letter)

1. Address, Salutation, and Thanksgiving 1:1–9
2. Concerning Disunity 1:10–4:21
   a. Dissension in the church 1:10–17
      (Related to boasting of special knowledge received in baptism)
   b. God's wisdom *vs* worldly (i.e., Corinthian) wisdom 1:18–2:16
   c. Paul preaches God's secret and Spirit-given wisdom 2:6–16
   d. Factions among the self-proclaimed wise (mature) 3:1–23
   e. The church's judgment of Paul 4:1–21
3. Problems of Immorality 5:1–6:11
   a. A case of incest 5:1–13
   b. A lawsuit between Christians 6:1–11
4. Reply to Questions in the Corinthians' Letter to Paul 6:12–16:12
   a. Introduction 6:12–20
   b. Concerning marriage 7:1–40
   c. Concerning idol meat 8:1–11:1
   d. Concerning distinctions between men and women [7] 11:2–16
   e. Reply to oral report of unseemly behavior at the congregational meal 11:17–34
   f. Concerning spiritual gifts 12–14
   g. Concerning the resurrection 15
   h. Concerning the collection 16:1–4
5. Paul's Travel Plans 16:5–9
6. News of Timothy's Visit 16:10–11
7. Concerning Apollos 16:12
8. Conclusion 16:13–22
   a. Closing paraenesis (ethical instruction) 16:13–18
   b. Closing greeting, apostolic warning, and benediction 16:19–24

OUTLINE OF 2 CORINTHIANS 10:1–13:13 (Paul's Third Letter)[8]

1. Address, Salutation, and Thanksgiving   Lost
2. Defense of the Authority of His Apostleship 10
   a. Rejection of the charge of cowardice 10:1–6
   b. Reply to the charge of weakness 10:7–11
   c. Defense of his right to "boast" 10:12–18

3. Concerning Justifiable Boasting 11:1–12:13
   a. Reason for this foolish indulgence 11:1–6
   b. Response to the charge of refusing money 11:7–15
   c. Plea to accept the folly of his boasting 11:16–21
   d. Paul's boasting rooted in suffering and weakness 11:22–12:10
   e. Conclusion 12:11–13
4. Concerning Paul's Imminent Visit 12:14–13:10
   a. Announcement of visit 12:14–18
   b. Paul's fear of finding Corinthians unrepentant 12:19–21
   c. Sharp apostolic warning 13:1–10
5. Conclusion 13:11–13

OUTLINE OF 2 CORINTHIANS 1–9 (minus 6:14–7:1) (Paul's Fourth Letter)
1. Address, Salutation, and Thanksgiving 1:1–11
2. Autobiographical Report and Apology 1:12–2:17
   a. Sincerity of the apostle 1:12–14
   b. Reason for postponement of apostolic visit 1:15–2:4
   c. Treatment of the offender 2:5–11
   d. Report on his ministry from Troas to Macedonia 2:12–17
3. Defense of Paul's Apostolic Ministry 3:1–6:10
   a. Others need letters of recommendation but "you are our letter of recommendation" 3:1–3
   b. Others claim sufficiency but our sufficiency is from God who appointed "us" as ministers of the new covenant 3:4–11
   c. Truth of Scripture veiled to others; for "us" Christ lifts the veil from the Scriptures 3:12–18
   d. Others preach themselves; "we" preach Christ 4:1–6
   e. Others validate preaching with manifestations of glory; we validate ours through suffering 4:7–5:10
   f. Others pride themselves on their "position" but the "love of Christ controls us" 5:11–6:2
   g. Final appeal to recognize the manifestation of God in his suffering, weakness, etc. 6:3–10
4. Invitation to Reconciliation 6:11–7:16
   a. Plea to restore relationship 6:11–13; 7:2–4
   b. Report of Titus on Corinthian visit with a parenthesis on the severe letter 7:5–16
5. The Collection for the "Poor" in Jerusalem 8–9
   a. Example of the churches in Macedonia 8:1–6
   b. Appeal to share in the offering 8:7–15
   c. Titus and others commissioned to assist 8:16–24
   d. Exhortation to prepare 9:1–5
   e. Exhortation to give generously 9:6–15
6. Conclusion   Lost

GALATIANS (ca. A.D. 54–56)

Paul founded the Galatian church[9] from a sickbed. When illness overtook him on his way through Galatia, the local people took him in and nursed him back to health (4:13–16). During his recuperation, and perhaps after, Paul spoke to the Galatian gentiles of their adoption as sons of God. No longer, he said, did they need to be slaves of this world's hostile, demonic powers (4:8–9). Through the crucified one and the gift of the Holy Spirit, liberation was offered from their pagan gods. After hearing this "good news" and witnessing the mighty deeds of Paul (3:5), the Galatians received his gospel with enthusiasm and revered the apostle himself. Their patient had become their savior; an "angel of God," even Jesus Christ himself they called him (4:14). Their devotion was so extreme that they would, if possible, have given him their eyes (4:15).

1. OPPOSITION DEVELOPS

At Paul's departure all was well. Some time later, however, he learned that the Galatians were adopting another version of the gospel. His apostleship was under attack, and the church was in turmoil. Whether the opposition to Paul was inspired by outsiders or led by insiders is hotly debated. In any case, the nature of the opposition is clear. Since Paul had left Galatia his converts there had learned from Jewish Scriptures that the promises of God belong to the children of Abraham, and that one becomes a son of Abraham through circumcision. Abraham, the father of many gentiles (Gen. 17:5), received circumcision when 99 years old after having received God's promise. Likewise, the Galatians might well have reasoned, it was necessary for them, the spiritual descendants of Abraham, to receive circumcision. Such a conclusion would have been natural in light of Genesis 17:10 which reads, "This is my covenant, which you shall keep, between me and you and your descendants after you: Every male among you shall be circumcised." Later in Genesis 17:14 divine proscription is placed on those who disobey the command: "Any uncircumcised male who is not circumcised . . . shall be cut off from his people." Word of the observance of circumcision by the Jewish Christians in Jerusalem may have strengthened the belief of the Galatians that they, too, should be circumcised. For whatever reason, by the time Paul writes our letter, the Galatians are requiring all baptized males to be circumcised (5:2, 11; 6:12–13). Their zeal for God and the Scriptures led them to keep other parts of the Law as well (3:2; 4:21; 5:4, 18).

The Galatians thus attempted to revise Paul's gospel by adding the Hebrew rite of circumcision. They also incorporated much from the local folk religion. They continued worshiping certain "elemental spirits" (4:9) and observing their sacred pagan festivals—"days, and months, and seasons, and years." (4:10)

Of a piece with the modification of Paul's gospel were the questions raised about Paul himself. It was impossible to separate the credibility of the message from the integrity of the messenger. The Galatians began to wonder, what else was Paul but an interloper into the apostolic circle? Jesus' original followers, even Jesus' brother James, were leaders in the Jerusalem church. Their link with the Lord was personal and the authority for their leadership was unquestioned. Paul, however, was a johnny-come-lately, for it was only after Jesus' death that Paul learned of Jesus and his followers, and then only as their adversary. How could he claim to be the Lord's apostle when he had not known him? His tradition had come from followers of Jesus, not Jesus himself. Thus, in the Galatian view, Paul's gospel was secondhand and deficient. However good his intentions or impressive his preaching, Paul's gospel required an additive. It was necessary to supplement the apostle's message with a version of the gospel wider in scope, stricter in discipline, more firmly grounded on Scripture and apostolic tradition. It is possible that their appeal to the Law was developed partly in opposition to certain religious enthusiastic tendencies in the church which had resulted from Paul's preaching of salvation by grace alone. Note, however, Galatians 5:13ff. where Paul himself warns against "freedom in the Spirit," i.e., insensitivity to any distinction between moral and immoral behavior.

2. WHO WERE PAUL'S OPPONENTS?

a. Scholars hold three views on the identity of Paul's opponents. One view is that Jewish Christians from Jerusalem, possibly from the Peter or James circle, trailed Paul from place to place seeking to correct his misrepresentation of the gospel. The theory is that the Jewish Christian church in Jerusalem kept the Law, and sought to impose it on Paul's congregations which believed in justification by grace apart from the Law. This view suffers from the lack of any reference or allusion to such opposition in Paul's letter. Although Paul was eager to show his independence of "the pillars" in Jerusalem, he nevertheless reports their endorsement of his gospel (2:9–10). If the pillars endorsed Paul's gospel, it is unlikely that they would then actively oppose it. Moreover, the Galatian charge that Paul was dependent on the Jerusalem church for his gospel makes no sense at all if the Jerusalem leaders were opposing him. And if Paul's opponents were Jewish Christians from Jerusalem, it is puzzling he should have to remind them that one who submits to circumcision is obligated to keep the whole Law. Any Jewish Christian from Jerusalem would have known that—it was an ancient Pharisaic principle, and it is not likely they would have neglected it. Finally, the reversion of the Galatians to the service of "elemental spirits" (4:9) and their tendency to turn Christian freedom into libertinism (5:13) could hardly have been the result of a campaign by Jewish Christians to bring all of Paul's converts to obedience to the Law.

b. Followers of Johannes Munck, a distinguished Danish scholar, hold that Paul's opponents were members of the Galatian congregation.[10] Munck pointed out that Paul refers to the troublemakers as "those who are being circumcised" (6:13, author's translation) which would be singularly inappropriate if it were meant to refer to Jews from Jerusalem—who, of course, had been circumcised long ago. On Munck's side also is the absence of a single reference to the opponents as "outsiders" (unlike 2 Cor. 10–13). In support of Munck's view, Lloyd Gaston has shown that, oddly enough, there were gentile Judaizers in Asia Minor, although in a somewhat later period.[11] We must allow Ignatius (Ign. Phila. 6:1) to speak in his own words: "If anyone interpret Judaism to you do not listen to him; for it is better to hear Christianity from the circumcised [such as Paul] than Judaism from the uncircumcised [gentile Judaizers]."[12] It would be natural enough for gentile converts to conclude from reading Jewish Scripture than circumcision was required of all believers (see Gen. 17:11, 25). Inevitably, this practice would cause some to wonder why Paul had not required circumcision. Paul's silence on this issue would have been especially perplexing in light of the practice of circumcision in the Jewish Christian church in Jerusalem. Had Paul deliberately misrepresented the gospel he got from Jerusalem by omitting the circumcision requirement? The issue is complicated by the fact that Paul, unlike Peter and James, had not known the earthly Jesus. Could it be, the Galatians may have asked, that the gospel of the pillars is more authentic than Paul's gospel?

Although Munck has raised important questions about the identity of Paul's opponents, many scholars feel his thesis does not account for the references to behavior having nothing to do with Jewish faith and practice. It is especially difficult to square Munck's thesis with the references to worship of elemental spirits, observance of days, months, seasons, and years and to libertine behavior.

c. Walter Schmithals, a noted German scholar, argues that Paul's Galatian converts were syncretists. Combining certain features from Jewish practice (like circumcision) with items drawn from their own folk religion, they tried to accommodate Paul's gospel to their own religious and social context. Such a thesis allows for the amateurism that characterized the Galatian observance of circumcision. One is struck by their unawareness of the principle that this cultic act obligated them to keep the entire Law. But it seems strange, if it was syncretism which threatened the integrity of Paul's gospel, that he should give so little space to the threat of the local folk religion, and so much to the Judaizing menace. In our discussion we have adopted a variation of this third option.

3. PAUL'S RESPONSE

The attempts to undermine Paul's apostleship and supplement his gospel evoked a fiery rejoinder. In place of the usual warm, friendly thanksgiving, Paul opens with an angry outburst—"I am astonished that you are so quickly deserting him who called you in the grace of Christ." (1:6) He then proceeds to call down a curse from heaven on the heads of his rivals preaching another gospel (1:7–9). And later, he excoriates those who take delight in circumcising others and suggests in disgust that they mutilate themselves

(5:12). He even tells those who receive circumcision that they are severed from Christ (5:4). Finally, he warns those who attack him that it is really Christ they oppose (6:17).

It may seem strange to the modern reader that Paul would link the defense of his apostleship with the defense of his gospel. But for Paul and his readers the integrity of his apostolic commission and the truth of his gospel were inseparable. It is clear then why the letter opens with Paul's defense of his apostleship. The Galatians charge that Paul's gospel came from man, that is from the leaders of the Jerusalem church (1:11). Paul, however, insists that since the time of his call he has been independent of the Jerusalem church. For three years after his call he did not so much as visit Jerusalem, and when he finally did, it was only for 15 days. And he did not return to Jerusalem again for 14 years. Moreover, he insists, even during his brief time in Jerusalem he maintained his independence, gained acceptance for his gospel, and on one occasion publicly rebuked Peter for his duplicity on the issue of eating with gentiles. By arguing that Christ, not the Jerusalem leaders, commissioned him directly, Paul wants to break free of the charge that he is dependent on the Jerusalem "pillars" for his gospel (see 1:18–2:21).

Paul begins his defense of his gospel by appealing to Scripture. His discussion centers on Abraham, a figure who was important both to the apostle and the Galatians. As a Jew, Paul was a son of Abraham according to the flesh (Rom. 4:1; 11:1). Abraham was also the patron of all proselytes, since God's promise was that through him all the nations (i.e., gentiles) would be blessed. It is likely that the Galatians shared Paul's interest in the Abraham narrative, for in it they would have found grounds for requiring circumcision. After receiving the covenant Abraham and all of his descendants were commanded to undergo circumcision (Gen. 17:9–11). Any male who remained uncircumcised would "be cut off from his people." (Gen. 17:14) Against this interpretation of the Abraham narrative Paul appeals to Genesis 15:6 which says Abraham "*believed* the LORD; and he [i.e., the Lord] reckoned it to him as righteousness" (italics added). Therefore, Paul concluded, since Abraham was counted righteous on account of his faith before he was circumcised, it is faith, not circumcision which links the children of promise with Abraham.

In Galatians 3:16 Paul employs a method of Scripture interpretation which some might think grotesque. There he says,

> Now the promises were made to Abraham and to his offspring. It does not say, "And to offsprings," referring to many; but, referring to one, "And to your offspring," which is Christ.

Given the benefit of modern exegetical methods, we know, of course, that Paul is unfaithful here to the original intent of the Genesis material. But it is unfair to expect him to use modern, sophisticated techniques in his interpretation of Scripture. His rabbinic methods were second nature and automatically went into play here to support his conviction that on the last day God would gather people from all quarters of the world, Jew and gentile, to form the new holy community. Significantly, Paul argues that since the promise is to Abraham's seed (*zera'*, sing., i.e., Christ), it is through faith in Christ, not observance of Law, that gentiles become true sons of Abraham.

In light of his more positive statements about the Law elsewhere, Paul's almost totally negative picture of it in Galatians is disturbing. The statements here must be read as exaggerations for effect—a polemical attempt to confute the Galatian revisionists. Paul opposes their effort to supplement his gospel with observance of Law for two reasons: (1) It reveals a fundamental distrust in the adequacy of his gospel and the God who gave it. In Jerusalem Paul had successfully defended his right to offer full salvation to gentiles. He believed in the full right of gentiles as gentiles to be equal members of the people of God. Now Paul's critics were suggesting that gentiles who entered the church through grace instead of the Law were second-class citizens. If they were to become *full* members of the elect community, they must receive circumcision. To Paul this addition was no mere minor change but a fundamental repudiation of the gospel of salvation by grace. (2) In Paul's view the Galatian experiment with the Law was amateurish. One senses Paul's disdain, if not contempt, for those who think they can keep selected portions of the Law. Paul reminds the Galatians of a basic Pharisaic principle that evidently they have overlooked: "every man who receives circumcision . . . is bound to keep the *whole* law" (5:3, emphasis added). Paul says this, however, not to urge those who are keeping only a part of the Law to keep all 613 commandments, but to encourage his listeners to claim full membership in God's kingdom by grace and not as righteous proselytes via Judaism.[13] Since the Galatians came to enjoy life in the Spirit through "hearing with faith" free from "works of the Law" Paul would have them continue in the way of responsible freedom (ch. 5).

OUTLINE OF GALATIANS

1. Address and Salutation 1:1–5
2. Expression of Astonishment [14] 1:6–9
   (Instead of Thanksgiving)
3. Paul's Defense of His Apostleship 1:10–2:21
4. Paul's Defense of His Gospel 3–4
   a. Spirit comes through gospel not Law 3:1–5
   b. Law and faith 3:6–29
      Example of Abraham as father of promise and a discussion of the nature of Law and its relationship to faith.
   c. Law and grace 4
      Adopted sons are not slaves to the Law. Inferiority of way of Law to way of grace for gentiles as illustrated by the allegory of Hagar and Sarah.

5. The Gospel Applied: the Responsible Use of Christian Freedom 5–6
  a. Stand fast in freedom 5:1–12
  b. Freedom to love 5:13–25
  c. The law of Christ 5:26–6:10
6. Personal Exhortation and Conclusion 6:11–18

ROMANS (*ca.* A.D. 55–57)

1. INTEGRITY OF THE LETTER

There are, or once were, three different manuscript versions of Romans—one ending with chapter 14, one with chapter 15, and one with chapter 16. But which one went to the church of Rome? The scholarly consensus is that it was not the bobtailed edition (chs. 1–14 and the benediction 16:25–27). This short version was used if not created by Marcion, a second-century heretic. Given his tendency to take the knife to disagreeable texts and given his distaste for the Old Testament, Marcion may have been inspired by Paul's praise of the Old Testament in 15:4 and his positive use of it in 15:9–12, 21 to amputate the entire chapter and add his own benediction (16:25–27). Since short versions of the letter do surface, however, in a few late Latin manuscripts, it is possible that Marcion adopted but did not father the short form of the letter.

Arguments that the long version (chs. 1–16) went to Rome raise a host of questions. Would Paul have known 26 Christians in Rome whom he could greet by name (16:3–15)? Since in the other letters he greets no addressee by name, one might wonder whether, even had he known 26 Christians in Rome, he would have greeted them. Prisca and Aquila were working with Paul in Ephesus when 1 Corinthians 16:19 was written. Had they now returned to Rome? Paul greets Andronicus and Junias (Rom. 16:7), who were in prison with him, presumably in Ephesus. Had they also moved to Rome? Paul calls Epaenetus "the first convert in *Asia*" (16:5 italics added) but now he also is in Rome—if chapter 16 is a part of the original letter. While such a mass movement of Paul's acquaintances to Rome is not impossible, it is not likely. More important than the greetings, however, is Paul's stern warning against false doctrine in 16:17–19. From all that we know, such an injunction squares less with the Roman milieu than with the situation in the eastern church (e.g., see 2 Corinthians and Philippians).[15]

More tenable is the view that Paul's original letter to Rome contained only chapters 1–15 plus a concluding benediction which was removed to make way for chapter 16. Chapter 16 is a later work, perhaps by Paul himself, and was probably sent to a church in the East. Ephesus is the leading candidate for that honor. Even if chapter 16 were written at the same time as chapters 1–15, it was not a part of the same letter and should not be used to ascertain anything about the Roman situation. We will assume here that the original letter contained only chapters 1–15.

2. BACKGROUND OF THE ROMAN CHURCH

We do not know who founded the Roman church or when. We know only that it had already been in existence "for many years" before Paul wrote Romans (15:23), and that there was a church in Rome before A.D. 49, the year the Emperor Claudius "expelled from Rome the Jews who were constantly stirring up a tumult under the leadership of Chrestus" (Suetonius, "Claudius," 25, in *The Lives of the Twelve Caesars*).

Although Suetonius' report is vague it probably refers to heated or even violent arguments in the Jewish community concerning Christ. Aquila and Prisca, Paul's co-workers in Corinth (1 Cor. 16:19), conceivably were among those expelled by Claudius. Meanwhile the gentile Christians remained in Rome unmolested by the ban of Claudius. After the death of Claudius the ban was lifted (A.D. 54), and Jewish Christians were free to return to Rome once more. But the return of these Jewish Christians brought new tensions to the Roman church.

3. PROBLEM WITHIN THE CHURCH

Scholars disagree over the purpose of Romans. Perhaps no single reason is sufficient to explain its existence. In chapter 14 at least, Paul is aware of conflict between Jewish and gentile Christians and seeks to address that problem. Apparently the gentile emphasis on justification by grace apart from works of the Law had encouraged certain licentious tendencies in the church. Moreover, returning Jewish Christians or Jewish converts would have been offended by the suggestion that the observance of dietary rules and the Christian gospel were incompatible. Some gentile Christians may have argued that the church had replaced Israel and therefore Jewish Christians were obligated to quit their hallowed traditions (see 9–11).

In all likelihood Jewish Christians were offended that gentiles would think observance of Jewish dietary laws was a refusal of salvation apart from works of the Law (see ch. 14). In spite of the disdain of their gentile brothers and sisters, these Jewish Christians preferred eating no meat at all (14:2) to eating that not kosher. Jewish Christians would also have abstained from the wine which was routinely offered to pagan gods before its sale (14:21). Eating the food of the pagan gods or drinking their wine in Jewish tradition was to be guilty of idolatry (14:3). Naturally, in their view, it was better to be a *Jewish* Christian—obedient to Torah, even at the risk of being overly scrupulous—than to be led into immorality through a gospel of justification by grace alone. Abraham, in their view, had shown that faith and the observance of Law are compatible, for he kept the whole Law even before it was written. Moreover, enough immorality existed among gentile Christians to cause these Jewish Christians to wonder if rejection of the Law had encouraged lawlessness.

In Romans Paul answers a number of Jewish objections to his gospel. "Are we to continue in sin that grace may abound?" (6:1) "Are we to sin because we are not under law but under grace?" (6:15) Is the law sin (7:7)? If God has turned to the gentiles away from his chosen people, have his promises failed (9:6)? Paul was in a unique position to answer these questions, because they had all been hurled at him before. Most Jewish Christians, like Paul, were active in both synagogue and church, and were thus continually exposed to ridicule and harrassment from non-Christian Jews. Thus, the same Jewish Christians who were accused by gentile Christians of being overly scrupulous in the observance of Law, were charged by the synagogue leaders with abandoning it. Why, these leaders might ask, do not the gentiles first become proselyte Jews if they wish to become heirs of the promise? Moreover, some Jewish Christians had abandoned the synagogue altogether, claiming to be "not under law but under grace." (6:15) What kind of gospel was this that caused men to jettison the Law and begin the gradual slide into immorality? Incredulously they asked, how could anyone keep God's Law and also accept a gospel which rejected the Law as unnecessary?

4. PAUL'S RESPONSE

Paul wrote Romans, unlike other letters, to a church he had neither founded nor visited. In Romans Paul names no adversary and attacks no opponent. Yet, like his other epistles, Romans is a genuine letter, not a treatise in systematic theology. Although its depth of insight is great, some would say unsurpassed, it nevertheless has the structure of a letter, conveys the warmth of a truly personal correspondence, and addresses a particular situation.

Written on the heels of Paul's heated exchange with the Corinthian and Galatian churches, Romans echoes many of the concerns in those letters. But Romans is also quite definitely distinct from them, and is by no means, as several have suggested, simply a calm, reflective summary of the wisdom Paul gained in his turbulent dealing with the Corinthian and Galatian churches. In this letter Paul neither mentions Judaizers (Galatians) nor Gnostic enthusiasts (Corinthians and Philippians). The Roman church is troubled, but it is not heretical. As Paul says, "I myself am satisfied about you, my brethren, that you yourselves are full of goodness, filled with all knowledge, and able to instruct one another." (15:14) About some things, however, Paul wants to strengthen them and be strengthened by them (1:11–12). He hopes to reconcile a divided church and build a base from which to launch his mission to Spain (15:24, 28). Since he has never visited the church, the situation is delicate. The gentile majority might resent his intrusion in their affairs. The Jewish Christian minority, after hearing that Paul was a dangerous innovator, might be less than overjoyed at the prospect of a visit from him. In the discussion below we see how carefully Paul addresses the Roman situation.

After the long introduction (1:1–17) Paul reminds his audience that the coming of Christ exposed the historical failure of both Jews and gentiles either to do the will of God or to render the thanks due him. Therefore, Paul asserts, boasting by the Jew and arrogance by the gentile are both excluded: "all have sinned and fall short of the glory of God" (3:23), and all stand in equal need of God's grace (3:24). Paul's gospel appeared to some Jews to be a pernicious provocation. If man's sin elicits God's grace, why not do more evil that more good may come? (3:8) Paul's gospel was suspect on two counts: (1) His mission to the gentiles raised questions about God's credibility. Had God now reneged on his promise to Abraham and his seed (i.e., the Jews) by going to someone else? (2) The gospel of grace outside the Law encouraged immorality by suggesting that morality didn't matter.

Paul defends himself against both charges. He first argued that gentiles who believe *are* the real sons of Abraham who also was counted righteous because of his faith. Before turning to the charge of libertinism Paul uses the analogy of Adam to show how one man's act can affect the destiny of all mankind. Just as through one man, Adam, sin was introduced into the human context to the detriment of all so now through one man, Jesus, acquittal and life are offered to *all* (Jew and gentile).

In chapter six Paul returns to the question raised in 3:8. If human sin elicits God's grace then why not sin in order that grace may be multiplied?

Paul was especially touchy over the charge that his gospel encouraged immorality as a means of receiving grace. In Corinth and Philippi at least, some had understood salvation by grace outside the Law to mean that all things were lawful. In those cities certain libertines seemed to anticipate Herod's caricature of grace found in W. H. Auden's *For the Time Being:* "I like committing crimes. God likes forgiving them. Really the world is admirably arranged." [16] Drawing on three images—baptism, slavery, and marriage—Paul asks how anyone who shares in the life of the new age can still act as if he were a member of the old. In baptism, Paul argues, the Christian dies to sin. How, therefore, can anyone continue to live in it (6:1–14)? How can those freed from sin to become slaves of righteousness revert to the old slavery (6:15–23)? A woman is freed after the death of her husband to remarry. So Christians who have died to the Law through Christ now belong to another. How, therefore, can they still act as if the old marriage was in effect (7:1–6)? Drawing on these images Paul wants to correct the impression that his gospel encourages immorality by pointing to the new obedience effected in Christ.

Upon broaching the subject of the Law Paul hears the Jewish Christian (7:1) asking if the Law is sinful (7:7). The Jews had called the Law God's gift to Israel. To call the gift "evil" would raise questions about the nature of God himself. Is his will so dark and his nature so sinister that he gives malevolent gifts to his children? It is man's crooked heart, Paul submits, which twists the Law into a grotesque caricature, not the Law that is evil. The Law may forbid one to "covet" (7:7) but it is the nature of man to covet most what is forbidden. The fault is not in the Law or God who gave it, but in the creature himself. It is the misuse of the Law, not the Law itself which, Paul says, will "bring death." (7:13) Two problems face us in 7:13–25: (1) The ambiguity of the term "flesh" (*sarx*) and (2) uncertainty about how Paul is using the term "I." As a faithful Jew Paul would have been unable to attribute evil to the flesh *per se*. Flesh, for the Jew, was morally neutral, but it was, nevertheless, humankind's Achilles heel. Through the flesh and the desires associated with it, mankind was vulnerable to sin's attack. After gaining a foothold the evil impulse (*yetzer*) takes up residence in man's flesh and corrupts him. It is possible for the flesh to be corrupted but it is not in and of itself a corrupting element. Paul does mean his "flesh" when he refers to the corrupted element ("nothing good dwells within me"), but when he does so he is not saying that the physical is inherently perverse but that the person has fallen victim to the power of sin. When Paul speaks of those who live "according to the flesh" (8:12) he is referring to those whose flesh has been taken captive by the diabolical force in the world, but in the strictest sense the term "flesh" carries no negative charge.

The second problem concerns Paul's use of the term "I" in 7:7–25. His use of the first person singular coupled with the past tense, and the apparent parallel Paul draws between his own development and that of Adam (man) in the Genesis narrative, suggest that Paul may be referring to his own personal experience in this section. It is more likely, however, that Paul, here as in 1 Corinthians 13, uses the first person singular to speak not just of his own experience but representatively of all mankind. Therefore, the passage probably should not be read as an autobiographical statement about the anxiety and depression Paul suffered trying to keep the Law. In Philippians 3:4ff. he suggests, on the contrary, that he was blameless before the Law. It is simply that the coming of Christ has fundamentally altered Paul's former view that salvation came through the Law.

In chapters 9–11 Paul answers a barrage of questions raised by his mission to the gentiles: Does this mission undermine the promises God made to Israel? If God made promises to Israel but has now turned to the gentiles, has his plan failed? Has he welched on his promises (9:6)? One might reply, Paul says, that God has always chosen to bless some and not others; for example, he preferred the younger son Joseph over his older brothers. He chose Jacob over Esau, etc. Could he not do the same by turning to the gentiles instead of Israel? If such a natural selection process is operative then the question arises, is it fair for God arbitrarily to reject the chosen and choose the rejected (9:14)? Furthermore, if it is God who hardens hearts or makes them receptive, how can he find fault with the Jews for rejecting Jesus (9:19)? Finally, if the gentiles who did not pursue righteousness receive it through faith, will the Jews who did pursue righteousness be excluded from God's plan of salvation? If so, is God just? In answer to these questions, Paul argues for the validity of his gentile mission. At the same time he insists that God has not forsaken Israel. It is Paul's conviction that both the gentiles *and* Israel will be brought together in God's final eschatological community (11:29–32). In an aside found in 11:13–24, Paul warns his gentile converts against presumption: "For if God did not spare the natural branches [i.e., Jews], neither will he spare you." (11:21)

Paul was alive to the charge that his gospel of salvation apart from the Law encouraged immorality. By means of analogy he has already argued that license is inconsistent with his gospel of freedom (Rom. 6). Now in Romans 12–15 he deals with the issue more directly. Throughout the section Paul develops an ethical imperative consistent with the gospel he preaches.[17] He admonishes all who have special gifts—prophets, teachers, leaders, administrators, etc.—to use their gifts for the nurture and the reconciliation of the church. He urges believers to love outsiders—"Bless those who persecute you," "repay no one evil for evil," "associate with the lowly," "never avenge yourselves," and "if your enemy is hungry, feed him . . . ." (12:14–21) This preoccupation with the outsider flows into Paul's discussion of the believers' relationship to "governing authorities" in 13:1–10.

An additional word is necessary because of the influence this passage has had on the Christian view of the state throughout the centuries. At the beginning we should ask if or how the discussion in 13:1–10 is related to Paul's wider epistolary purposes. Already Paul has stated that Jesus is the head of a new humanity (5:18), and is the new Lord (*Kurios*) for the believer (5:15–16 and 10:9). Paul was painfully aware that their membership in the arriving kingdom of God had led believers elsewhere to disregard the claims of this world (see 1 Thessalonians and 1 Corinthians). Perhaps believers in Rome had also abandoned the present, provisional order in favor of the new divine order soon to come. By withholding support (taxes, civil service, etc.) from the "earthly" kingdom, they could testify their loyalty to a kingdom not of this world. On the other hand, Paul may have been responding to the indictment that his gospel encouraged irresponsible if not immoral behavior.

Paul answers by reaffirming the otherworldly character of his gospel *along with* its worldly imperative. He tells the believers in Rome "Do not be conformed to this world" (12:2) but at the same time he says "Let every person be subject to the governing authorities" (13:1) and pay "taxes to whom taxes are due." (13:7) He reasserts his conviction that the day of the Lord is at hand (13:12), but the nearness of the hour does not cancel civic duty. It gives it cosmic significance. As the divine denouement nears, the opportunity for witness becomes more limited and the necessity for it becomes more urgent; the Christian is to sieze whatever opportunities avail to witness. The fact that the state provides an orderly society in which travel and witness can go on unimpeded, is not Paul's main point. More likely he is urging the Christian to use the civic realm as an arena in which the eschatological fruit of love receives concrete expression. This love of the neighbor (13:10) is to be expressed partly by support for "authorities": for such institutions reward the good (13:3) and punish evil (13:4) and thereby protect the neighbor.

Paul also argues that the "governing authorities" are ministers of God (13:4). Implicit in this statement is Paul's view that in the cross and resurrection God has not canceled his action in history. Instead he has begun his final stage of lordship over events. Loyalty to Jesus as Lord, therefore, is allegiance to one whose realm includes rather than excludes historical agents such as "the authorities." Hence, to abandon responsibility in this world, in Paul's view, means to retreat from the arena of God's activity. This hardly implies, however, that Paul espoused blind allegiance to the state. The primary claim in his view always belongs to God. But allegiance to God, Paul says, does not preclude giving to the state what properly belongs to it (taxes, honor to magistrates, and so on). One might wonder what Paul would have said had he lived to see the persecution by Nero ten years later.

In 14:1–15:13 Paul deals at great length with peace within the community of the faithful: "Welcome one another . . . as Christ has welcomed you" (15:7), etc. Gentiles are urged to respect the dietary scruples of Jewish Christians, and Jewish Christians are urged to refrain from harsh polemic against gentile Christians.

In the close of the letter, the western horizon of Paul's mission breaks into view. Paul writes, "I shall go on by way of you to Spain" (15:28, see also 1:13). With his eastern mission complete between Jerusalem and Illyricum (15:19), and the offering for the "poor among the saints" ready for delivery to Jerusalem (15:25–27), Paul's mind races to Rome and beyond to Spain. Paul obviously hopes that a strong, united church in Rome will share his vision of God's eschatological community and will include representatives of all peoples on earth, Jew and Greek, Galatian and Spaniard, slave and free, male and female. If they share this vision, his hope is that they will also share in his mission, as the Macedonian church had done for the mission in Greece (2 Cor. 11:9). But even while these hopes burned in his breast, Paul seemed to inkle what was to happen in Jerusalem. "The unbelievers in Judea" (Rom. 15:31), Paul feared, might cause trouble. If Luke's account is correct (Acts 21:27ff.), Paul's intuition was sound. Arrested while on his visit to Jerusalem to deliver the offering, Paul, as a Roman citizen, appealed to and was granted a trial in Rome. There his ship moored for the last time. There was no launching of the great western mission to Spain.

OUTLINE OF ROMANS
1. Address and Salutation 1:1–7
2. Thanksgiving 1:8–12
3. Autobiographical Introduction 1:13–17

4. God's Wrath Now Being Revealed 1:18–3:20
   a. Judgment on gentiles who have failed to honor the creator 1:18–2:16
   b. Judgment on Jews who have failed throughout history to keep the Law 2:17–3:20
5. God's Righteousness Now Being Revealed 3:21–5:21
   a. Righteousness comes through faith 3:21–31
   b. Abraham, patron of gentiles, justified by faith 4:1–25
   c. Righteousness (access, peace, reconciliation) comes through Jesus Christ 5:1–11
   d. How does the one man, Jesus, mediate righteousness? Just as through "First Adam" came sin and death so through Second Adam came acquittal, life, and grace 5:12–21
6. Questions about Libertinism 6:1–8:39
   a. If where sin abounds, grace abounds the more, why not sin that grace may abound?
      (1) Can those baptized into the new age still act as if they were in the old age? 6:1–14
      (2) Can those liberated from slavery still act as if they were slaves? 6:15–23
      (3) Can the woman whose husband (Law) has died and who becomes another man's wife (Christ's) go back to her former husband? 7:1–6
   b. If the Law is that from which one is liberated, is the Law, therefore, sinful? 7:7–25
   c. The Christian is not lawless—but walks by the law of the spirit of love in Jesus Christ 8:1–39
7. Questions and Answers about Israel's Place in Salvation History 9:1–11:30
   a. To Israel belong the promises, the messiah according to the flesh, etc. 9:1–5 If Israel rejects Jesus as the messiah and God turns to the gentiles, has God failed? 9:6–13
   b. If God selects some (gentiles) and rejects others (Israel) is God unjust? 9:14–18
   c. If God elects the gentiles, how can he find fault with Jews for resisting his will? 9:19–33
   d. God is not arbitrary—everyone, Jew and gentile, who calls on the Lord will be saved 10:1–21
   e. Has God rejected Israel? No! A remnant of Israel has accepted the gospel 11:1–10
   f. God has included gentiles in order to provoke Israel to jealousy so that Israel will accept the gospel 11:11–30
8. The Consequence of Life in the New Age 12:1–15:13
   a. Introduction (self-giving sacrifice) 12:1–2
   b. Behavior in the church 12:3–13
   c. Response to outsiders 12:14–21
   d. Response to the state 13:1–10
   e. Eschatological reinforcement 13:11–14
   f. The weak and the strong in Rome 14:1–15:13
9. Paul's Travel Plans 15:14–29
10. Conclusion 15:30–33

Since the conclusion of Romans has been tampered with, we no longer have the heavily stereotyped conclusion of the other letters. The doxology in 16:25–27 is almost universally recognized as a non-Pauline addition.

PHILIPPIANS (ca. A.D. 52–54 or 55–58)

Paul wrote to the Philippian church from a jail either in Ephesus (before 55) or in Rome (ca. A.D. 56–58).[18] From the time of its founding on, the Philippian church had a turbulent history. Paul spoke of the shameful treatment and fierce opposition he ran into there (1 Thess. 2:2). The church was hounded by outsiders (Phil. 1:29–30) and fractured by the pettiness and jealousy of insiders (3:2ff.; 4:2–3). Some there preached the gospel out of love and respect for Paul, and others preached it out of partisanship (1:15–17).

But throughout these strains and stresses the relationship between Paul and the Philippian church remained warm and deeply affectionate. The Philippians gave money to support Paul's mission in Thessalonica (4:16), and possibly also in Corinth (2 Cor. 11:9). They gave generously to the Jerusalem collection (2 Cor. 8:2–5) and they sent Epaphroditus to care for Paul in prison (Phil. 2:25). Paul had returned to Philippi on his way to Corinth (2 Cor. 2:13), and possibly again on his final visit to Jerusalem with the offering. And when in jail, Paul writes movingly of his love and longing for the Philippian Christians (4:1).

When Paul wrote the letter from prison, one hearing had already been held, and either Paul's condemnation (1:20; 2:17) or his release (1:25; 2:24) seemed imminent. His mission continued, however, in spite of the chains. Some, both inside and outside the praetorian guard, were touched by Paul's witness (1:13). Some of the slaves and freedmen from Caesar's household were converted (4:22). Through the courageous example of the apostle, some believers who were timid had become fearless (1:14). Word of Paul's imprisonment eventually leaked out to the congregation at Philippi, and considering their special reverence for Paul, the response was predictable. The exchanges which ensued may be reconstructed as follows:

1. Having learned that Paul was a prisoner in Ephesus, the Philippians sent Epaphroditus with money for his support and with instructions for his care.
2. Paul sent a letter of thanks (now lost?), and the bearer of this letter reported to the Philippians that Epaphroditus was very ill.
3. The Philippians wrote to Paul expressing:
    a. Their distress over Epaphroditus' critical condition (2:26)
    b. A request for the return of Epaphroditus and perhaps an expression of regret that his illness prevented him from serving Paul as they intended (2:25–30)
    c. Report of a quarrel between two women in the congregation, Euodia and Syntyche (4:2–5)

    d. Concern over the efforts of local Jews to win (back?) converts which the church had gained from the god-fearers (3:2–16)

    e. Concern about libertines in the congregation (3:17–20).

4. Paul sent the present letter (in whole or in part) with Epaphroditus (2:25).[19]

5. A visit by Timothy to Philippi was planned. He was to report back to Paul (2:19–23).

6. Paul planned a visit to Philippi if or when he was released (2:24).

A. OPPOSITION AT PHILIPPI

Don't be afraid of your "opponents," Paul tells his readers (1:28). Who were these "opponents"? What were they doing? What were they saying about Paul? Where did they come from? Although no precise description of the outlook of the opponents is possible, the general contours of their thought can be seen. They nag gentile Christians to accept circumcision (3:2); they preach a partisan gospel deliberately designed to torment the imprisoned apostle (1:17). They reject the importance of the cross (3:18) in favor of the glorious resurrected life. And they make a fetish of self-indulgence— "their god is the belly." (3:19) Owing to the absence of any sustained discussion of the Law, it is unlikely that the opponents were Galatian type Judaizers. Given their proclamation of Christ (1:17), they could not be from the synagogue, although Jewish opposition did exist in another form. The "opponents" were probably a type of religious syncretist. To them Paul's gospel is just one ingredient among many in a religious potpourri. Circumcision was a Jewish sign and seal of the covenant. Initiation into the local mystery religion was also adopted, to allow the neophyte to pass directly and completely from death to immortal life. These, when added to Paul's gospel of grace and freedom in Christ, led to a very peculiar, not to say grotesque, configuration.[20]

An alternative view is that Paul addresses several types of opponents in this letter—Jews bent on winning back gentile god-fearers, those who had slipped into morally lax habits, and Christians critical of his gospel. Another suggestion is that Paul was slow to recognize the character of the opposition, and is thus somewhat confused in his response. Although both of these alternative views are tenable, they seem less persuasive than the first view. Given the range of Paul's opposition elsewhere, it is hardly likely that he would have misjudged his opponents here. Moreover, if several types of opponents exist, it is strange that the groupings are so indistinct in the letter itself.

B. PAUL'S RESPONSE

To those who claim total salvation in the present, Paul speaks of "full salvation" as only a future possibility. Paul underscores the provisional nature of present salvation when he writes of sharing Christ's "sufferings, becoming like him in his death" in order to "attain the resurrection" in the future

(3:10–11). To reinforce this point Paul adds, "not that I have already obtained this [resurrection] or am already perfect, but I press on to make it my own. . . . I press on toward the goal for the prize of the upward call of God. . . ." (3:12–14) Paul then calls on the Philippians to imitate him and thus by implication he rejects the view of those who claim too much here and now (3:15–17). His emphasis on the future not only undercuts the smug, it also reassures those now suffering humiliation and loss. They, like their Lord, can look forward to exaltation and triumph (see Paul's use of the ancient Christian hymn in 2:6–11).

In 3:4–9 many think Paul is rejecting his Jewish past: "Whatever gain I had [as a Jew], I counted as loss for the sake of Christ." (vs. 7) This statement, however, is really just part of Paul's polemic against the "dogs" who seek to modify his gospel and discredit him, by appealing to circumcision as the gateway to the new life for gentiles. Paul responds in total disgust at such an eclectic view. In Romans 9:1–5, on the other hand, Paul speaks most positively of his Jewish heritage:

> They are Israelites, and to them belong the sonship, the glory, the covenants, the giving of the law, the worship, and the promises; to them belong the patriarchs, and of their race, according to the flesh, is the Christ. (vss. 4–5)

In spite of the competing claims, internal strife, and external threats, there is a genuine warmth and human tenderness in Philippians that is refreshing compared to the sharp clashes in Galatians and Corinthians. Paul, we see, was not always the stormy combatant. He is also a towering figure whose confidence in the outcome of history enabled him to look past the immediate disturbances and irritations with confidence.

OUTLINE OF PHILIPPIANS

1. Introduction, Salutation, and Thanksgiving 1:1–11
2. Paul's Situation 1:12–26
   The effect of his imprisonment on the local church, and his own attitude toward the imprisonment.
3. Exhortation to Stand Firm Against Opponents Following the Model of Christ 1:27–2:18
   Note especially 2:6–11, a pre-Pauline hymn which gives important information on the development of Christology in the early church.
4. Announcement of Travel Plans 2:19–30
5. Exhortation to Persevere in the Struggle Against Judaizing Propaganda and Libertinism 3:2–4:1
6. Appeal for Harmony 4:2–9
7. Thanks for Gifts 4:10–20
8. Closing Greetings and Benediction 4:7; 21–23

PHILEMON (ca. A.D. 52–54 or 55–57)

Perhaps after stealing money (vs. 18), Onesimus, a slave, ran away from his rich Christian master, Philemon (vs. 5). By coincidence he met Paul in prison and was converted to Christ (vs. 10). Paul wanted to keep Onesimus with him, and, on the strength of his apostolic office, he felt entitled to do so. Instead, he returned Onesimus to his master along with this brief letter. Paul urges Philemon to restore Onesimus to his household and treat him like a "beloved brother" (vs. 16). He pleads with Philemon not to mete out the harsh punishment to which Onesimus was liable as a runaway slave and possible thief. Paul looks forward to his own imminent release from prison and a visit with Philemon. "Prepare a guest room for me," he says (vs. 22).

PLACE AND TIME OF WRITING

Colossians 4:9 refers to Onesimus traveling with Tychicus to Colossae. If Colossians was written by Paul, then Philemon must have lived in the neighborhood of Colossae, the destination of the travelers Onesimus and Tychicus. That is, assuming that the letter to the Colossian church and to Philemon were written about the same time and that the trip of Onesimus referred to in Colossians was the same one Paul speaks of in Philemon, the return of Onesimus to his owner. If Colossians is a genuine Pauline letter, then the date of Philemon and the location of the addressee would be the same as that of Colossians.

On the other side, the Pauline authorship of Colossians is questioned by many scholars. Indeed, it is possible that the references to Onesimus in Colossians may have been put there under influence from Philemon. It is better to plead ignorance and say we simply do not know where Philemon lived or where Paul was imprisoned when he wrote the letter. Ephesus and Rome are the strongest contenders, but by his own admission Paul was in prison many times in many places. If, however, Ephesus is taken as the place of the imprisonment mentioned here, then the date 54–56 is plausible. If Rome is taken, then 56–61 would be a safe guess.

We have come to the end of our discussion of the letters as conversations. We confined our treatment to letters whose authenticity is not seriously questioned, for in those it is easier to see that we are dealing with real letters, highly personal in nature, intensely particular in their discussion of problems, and essentially conversational (a talking *with* not *at* others). It is hoped that reading the letters as conversations will help us appreciate them as dynamic exchanges rather than static deposits of eternal truth waiting passively to be mined of their treasure.

5. Paul and His Myths

To THE PERSON on the street the term *myth* is synonymous with "fiction" or "untruth." Because the old stories about gods, devils, witches, and talking snakes seem quaint they are shelved, assigned a place with other relics from mankind's infancy. But could it be that myths from the archaic past do not reflect primeval ignorance and superstition so much as they reveal the heights and depths the human spirit can reach wrestling with questions about life and death, love and hate, fate and freedom, truth and falsehood? Could it be that myth and legend mirror not what happened in the ancestral period but rather the response in the soul to what happened? Even if unhistorical, could myth be, like art for Picasso, "a lie which makes us realize the truth"? As important as it is to know "what happened" in the ancient past, do we not also need to know how men and women responded to those happenings? Increasingly, anthropologists, historians of religion, and Biblical scholars are turning their scrutiny upon myth and legend, because mythological materials provide a living window on men and women of an earlier time giving expression to their inmost imaginings. Such expressions often sensitize us to the profundity and high originality of these people of old.

To avoid misunderstanding, we must distinguish myth from metaphor. The term *pig* is a graphic expression when applied to a male chauvinist, but it is hardly myth. When Paul calls himself a boxer who pummels his body into submission he is using metaphor; when he recites the Eucharistic formula, "this is my body," he is drawing on myth. Metaphor is descriptive language about an event, whereas mythological language is an event itself, transporting the participants into a zone of sacred time or space. The breaking of the bread is more than picture language about Jesus' execution, it is an avenue through which one enters the presence of the Redeemer figure and becomes "a contemporary disciple." [1]

No definition of myth will entirely do. Myth has been called a means of comprehending reality and of being apprehended by it; but this description is vague and too general. Frankfort describes myth as "a form of poetry which transcends poetry in that it proclaims a truth; a form of reasoning which transcends reasoning in that it wants to bring about the truth it proclaims; a form of action, of ritual behavior, which does not find its fulfilment in the act but must proclaim and elaborate a poetic form of truth." [2] Although Frankfort's statement is helpful and provocative, it is more a poem about a poem than it is a useful definition of myth. Gerardus van der Leeuw calls myth "a spoken word, possessing decisive power in its repetition." [3] Although myth, like all forms of communication, is tied to the word, can its power be restricted to the word? The three statements above are sufficient to show the difficulty of forging a satisfactory definition of myth. Because of this difficulty, most writers discuss instead myth's character and function. It is that approach which we will follow here.

1. THE WORLD VIEWED MYTHOLOGICALLY

In the first century, the relationship of both peasant and philosopher to the natural world was closely personal. Where we see a landscape stiff and mute, they saw a world sparkling with life. Where we see things passively waiting for our hands to put them to use, they saw "Thou's" actively forcing themselves on the human consciousness. Where we see an order defined by abstract laws, they saw both order and chaos as vehicles of will and intent. When the cloud rumbled or the wind roared they did so because they decided to, or because their master said, "Rumble!" or "Roar!"

Paul's experience of the non-human world was likewise a personal one. In Romans 8:22 he speaks of the world's participation in the final apocalyptic woes attending the birth of the new age. The earth's share of this wretchedness goes back to the dawn of creation when as an innocent bystander she was forced to bear a part of the pain that followed Adam's disobedience. Earthquakes and storms, plagues and drought, snakes and disease are signs of the futility and decay which nature suffered because her destiny was linked from the very beginning with the destiny of humankind. The natural world, however, shares not only the agony but also the ecstasy of man. For God is now acting not only to redeem his wayward creature but also his burdened creation. Now that her redemption is near, the creation stands on tiptoe waiting to share in the liberation of the human and non-human world (8:19–21).

All through the ages the creation has worn an image of its creator. In spite of its distorted nature, the image of God's power and deity has remained recognizable. Notwithstanding mankind's efforts to deface the image, the marks of God's power and deity have never been completely erased (Rom. 1:20). The gentiles have always been able to recognize the fingerprints of the creator on his creation. Thus nature, like man, suffers from the alienation and dislocation which reach back to the primeval period; and nature, like man, continues to bear the image of its maker even if in a twisted form. We see that the alienation and hope which man and nature share make them kin.

In spite of this feeling of kinship, however, the world also seemed alien to Paul. He spoke of breaking through the barriers which restrict his existence either by ascending to the third heaven (2 Cor. 12:2), or of being delivered

from the struggles which attend life in the world (2 Cor. 5:8). He saw his
life unfolding in a world under the dominance of Satan (2 Cor. 4:4) and
he perceived the unsteadfast footing of that world—"the form of this world,"
he says, "is passing away." (1 Cor. 7:31) So Paul did not feel at home in the
world as it was but looked forward to the time when the original order would
be restored and all fear and dread between man and his world would be removed. As Paul says, "When anyone is united to Christ, there is a new world;
the old order has gone, and a new order has already begun." (2 Cor. 5:17,
NEB)

2. MYTH AND CULT

In the west we view time as an ever-flowing stream which bears its sons and
daughters away. But in the cult, time stands still. Time stops and is even reversed as the celebrant repeats the acts of God, or shares in the sacred deeds
of an earlier day.

In the celebration of the Passover today, for example, one sees Jewish
families who are indistinguishable from their neighbors in the clothes they
wear, the jobs they hold, or the cars they drive. Yet in recalling the deliverance of the Hebrews in Egypt thousands of years ago, they speak as if they
lived in the second millennium B.C. Drinking the wine and eating the un-
leavened bread, they see themselves as slaves in Egypt liberated from the
Pharaoh's bondage.

> We were Pharaoh's bondsmen in Egypt: and the Lord our God brought us
> out therefrom with a mighty hand and an outstretched arm. Now, if the
> Holy One, blessed be He, had not brought our fathers forth from Egypt,
> then we, and our children, and our children's children, would be servants
> to Pharaoh in Egypt.[4]

While to the outsider it may sound strange for an American Jew to speak
solemnly of sweating in Pharaoh's quarry long ago, to the insider who views
that bondage through the eyes of faith, the liberation which was effected
then is experienced once more.

Through the cultic act, the worshiper participates in what is real for all
time. While the key occurrences of both Judaism and Christianity are historical, for those within the traditions these events possess a vitality which
goes beyond the facts of the events themselves. As Jacob Neusner says, "If
'we, too, the living, have been redeemed,' then the observer no longer wit-
nesses only historical men in historical time, but an eternal return to sacred
time."[5] The great events which happened "once upon a time" continue to
direct the course of the world and are experienced as current. Through the
cult, the worshiper not only shares in the benefits of the primeval time, he
also finds an organizing center there for his disordered world.

The old shepherd ritualistically jumps over his staff three times; Mary
regularly calls for her four "friends" (stuffed animals) and her drink before

going to sleep; the Eskimo Emma Willoiya routinely bows her head to offer thanks both before and after eating her diet of raw fish. All are celebrating a tiny slice of life, and for each one, these gestures provide a structure for what otherwise would be an incoherent mass of activity. In myth also an order is imposed, but the order is not just any order but the true order, the only order that is fundamentally real. In the Hebrew experience of the exile we see how even the terrors of history were integrated into a divine order and were thus bearable because meaningful.

In 597 B.C. the Hebrews were uprooted from Palestine and deported to Mesopotamia. Eventually the temple was destroyed, the daily sacrifice interrupted, and Jerusalem left in shambles. Babylonian troops were garrisoned in the "promised land" while the Hebrew people raised the poignant cry, "How can we sing the Lord's song in a foreign land?" Yahweh had promised "the holy land" to his people Israel. Now Babylon had robbed Israel of her possession. Was Yahweh credible any more? Had God forsaken his people? Since Israel's whole existence had been defined in relation to Yahweh, what would happen if there was a break in that relationship? Would Israel languish and die at the feet of her captors, or would she survive to stand at their grave? The Hebrews found strength to face those hard times in worship, especially in the celebration of the Sabbath. The Babylonians could occupy the land; destroy the city; reduce the temple to dust; but they could not burn or destroy the Sabbath. On the Sabbath the Hebrews recalled how God had created the world out of formlessness and void, and how he had crowned his creation with the Sabbath itself (Gen. 1:1–2:4a). Thus, on each Sabbath the Hebrews celebrated an order that was real for all time, an order as old and fundamental as the creation itself. Nations might come and go, but this order always remained. Moreover, in each celebration of the Sabbath the Jews affirmed their faith that the God who in the beginning had brought order out of chaos would conquer the present historical chaos as well.

In Paul's letters also we see how the liturgy of the church serves as a bridge between the past and the present. In all of the early Christian churches baptism was used as the rite of initiation, and a sacred communal meal was eaten regularly—how regularly we do not know. In both these sacred rites the church shared in God's redemption of the world. Strangely enough, for Paul, the death and resurrection of Jesus rather than his teachings formed the glowing center of God's work. In passing through the water, and eating the bread and wine, the believer established a continuity between himself and the death which happened "once upon a time." In baptism the identification with Jesus is so complete that Paul can speak of being united with Christ in a death like his, of being baptized into his death (Rom. 6:3, 5) or even of being crucified with Christ (6:6). The immersion of the initiate in water simulated the burial of Jesus; the emergence of the initiate from the water imitated his resurrection. Through this rite the saving significance of the death and resurrection of Jesus was experienced within the community, and the believer was linked with that which is real for all time. As the spiritual says, in baptism the initiate *was* "there when they crucified my Lord."

Eliade's observation that "every ritual has a divine model" [6] applies to the Eucharist as well as to baptism. Throughout Paul's letters the eating of the bread and the drinking of the wine commemorate Jesus' last meal with his disciples. And the connection of this commemorative meal with the cross is so close that repetition of it spontaneously brings to mind Jesus' death. In 1 Corinthians 11:23ff., for example, Paul recites the Eucharistic tradition which he has received. Throughout the passage the emphasis is on death. Betrayal is mentioned. Bread is broken, simulating the breaking of Jesus' body, and the red wine is offered as the "new covenant in my blood." And finally to underscore the death motif Paul adds the exhortation, "as often as you eat this bread and drink the cup you proclaim the Lord's *death* until he comes." (11:26, italics added) To "proclaim the Lord's death" obviously extends beyond verbal announcement and means a mythic (or "spiritual") *participation* in the death as well.

Nevertheless, in 1 Corinthians 10:1–13 Paul counters the Corinthian belief that the Eucharist is a magic potion automatically guaranteeing salvation. He reminds the church that just as her life as the sacramental community was prefigured in Israel's wilderness wandering, so also was her punishment for any abuse of her status anticipated in the judgment of Israel. Israel's role as the sacramental family of God did not exempt her from the retribution of her Lord. Her murmuring brought capital punishment. Her immorality and idolatry brought the fall of 23,000 in a single day. Her tempting the Lord brought destruction by snakes. Likewise, Paul warns, being in the community of the saved exempts no one from God's judgment or condemnation. Believing their place in the sacramental community was absolutely sure, some Corinthians attended pagan feasts, perhaps with friends or relatives, assuming that they could do so without harm to themselves or the church. Appealing to their saved condition, the Corinthians felt they could participate in such pagan feasts and yet avoid fellowship with demons. Why, they might ask, should those who are already in the messianic age be intimidated by warnings of apostasy? Paul, however, thought flirtation with paganism arrogant and foolhardy. While to the modern reader Paul appears unnecessarily harsh in his remarks here, it is useful to remember that Paul saw the world as an arena of competing spheres of power. Understandably then Paul was worried when a Christian blithely entered the realm of demonic domination and participated: to do so was always to risk being attracted, in a deeply interpersonal way.

After citing the example of Israel, and warning the Corinthians to "shun the worship of idols" (1 Cor. 10:14), Paul introduces a reference to the Eucharist: "The cup of blessing which we bless, is it not a participation [*koinonia*] in the blood of Christ? The bread which we break, is it not a participation [*koinonia*] in the body of Christ?" (1 Cor. 10:16) The word *koinonia* is at present an "in" word, being used for everything from sensitivity groups to church campgrounds. When translated "fellowship," as is common, *koinonia* is taken to mean a spirit of jovial camaraderie. Ernst Käsemann has proposed a more accurate reading. He suggests that the word be rendered "falling into a sphere of domination." [7] And because this eating of the bread (flesh) and drinking of the wine (blood) places the Christian in the zone of the sacred, i.e., in the presence of the dead and risen Lord (1 Cor. 11:27–32), Paul must urge the Corinthians to purify themselves lest they profane the "body." Even perfunctory obeisance to demonic powers, as in the pagan sacrificial meals, was incompatible with participation in the body and blood of Christ. Because some believers persisted in attending the pagan sacrificial meals, however, and neglected to rid themselves of the taint of such unholy alliances, illness and even death had entered the community. This sickness and death, according to Paul, was not from natural causes but from the judging presence of the Lord in the cultic meal. In the solidarity with Christ effected in Eucharist, the believer even now foretasted the salvation or condemnation which would come in full at the end of the age.

The radicality of Paul is most obvious in the way he fixes on the death of Jesus as the locus of God's redeeming activity. In mythic participation in this death and resurrection, the believer already senses victory over the destructive, negative, and sinister elements in the world, and already shares in the reconciliation, love, and newness of the new creation. Intimations of the promise come through participation mythically in an event in the past. But the promise contained in that past event waits on the future for its full maturing. Thus, the past, brought mythologically into the present, becomes the basis of the future hope.

3. DEATH AS MODEL

Jesus' death functions in Paul not only as an earnest of God's plan, but also as a model for action in the world. In other words, Jesus' death is experienced not only in the cult but also in the daily round of work and play, eating and drinking, buying and selling, and making love and social intercourse. Paul frequently connects his own activity with the death of Jesus. Shipwreck, beatings, imprisonments, conflict and strife all serve as imitations of that death. Looking at the scars left by the "slings and arrows of outrageous fortune" Paul speaks of "carrying in . . . [his] body the death of Jesus." (2 Cor. 4:10) Injuries suffered in the service of the Lord are called "marks of Jesus" (Gal. 6:17)—an obvious allusion of his cuts to the wounds of crucifixion. Since the hunger, thirst, nakedness, homelessness, persecution, and slander Paul endured duplicated the suffering of Jesus, and since it was received in service to the Lord, Paul felt that his suffering shared in God's redemptive work. Even his hurt and pain inflicted by the world was shouldered for the sake of the world.

Drawing on his own experience, Paul urged the Corinthians to follow him and share "in Christ's sufferings" (2 Cor. 1:5). The Corinthian Christians, however, believed that they had already overcome the world, that they were "rich," "filled," and already ruling (1 Cor. 4:8), and therefore had no need to share the world's incompleteness. Believing themselves already saved, they celebrated their liberation from, not their participation in, suffering. By citing his own humiliation and deprivation, and calling on his converts to "be imitators of me," Paul abashed the claims of the Corinthians; he reminded them that neither their redemption nor the redemption of the world was complete. When Paul says, "I decided to know nothing among you except Jesus Christ and him crucified" (1 Cor. 2:2) he is trying to strip pretensions from the Corinthians and bring them to earth, so that they will see the reality of the world's hurt and the power of the cross (see 1 Cor. 1:17–25). As in 1 Thessalonians, so also in the Corinthian letter, Paul says suffering can be a symbol of honor, for it proclaims the affliction of the Lord: "You became imitators of us and the Lord, for you received the word in much affliction." (1 Thess. 1:6) In contrast, those who reject Paul's example and indulge themselves are called "enemies of the cross of Christ." (Phil. 3:17–18) It is not that sex or food are evil, but that preoccupation with them renders believers incapable of accepting either the suffering or the power that accompanies the way of the cross. It is possible that the sexual excesses and the gluttony at Philippi came of accommodating the gospel to old pagan ways, but most scholars believe they sprang from a perversion of Christian freedom. In Paul's view God had revealed himself in the cross. Now the transforming power of that moment was to be apprehended anew as it was remembered in both liturgy and the commonplace.

4. THE POWERS THAT BE

Although science has ostensibly freed us, superstition and fear, demons, monsters, wormlike and larval beasts live on in our collective fantasy. Goblins and witches come out on All Hallow E'en (Halloween); crepe paper dragons snake their way down city streets in popular parades; monster movies punctuate weekly television calendars; and mutant, bizarre creatures stalk the pages of science fiction. Despite our scientific better judgments, our fascination with these mythological beings persists. That fascination, however, surfaces only sporadically, mostly in our moments of corporate play or personal dreams. For Paul, however, contact with such powers was real, insistent and dreadful. The Devil, the superhuman rulers of this world-age, the elemental spirits of the universe, the principalities and powers, the beasts at Ephesus, Death, Sin, and pagan deities all lived, and contended for dominion of the world and the loyalty of mankind.

The Devil, for example, was an uncanny force, preying on the unsuspecting (1 Cor. 7:5), seeking to gain advantage over Paul (2 Cor. 2:11), and putting to death those excommunicated from the church, the realm of the rule of Christ (1 Cor. 5:5). Likewise, Death for Paul was a personalized power threatening God's purpose, paying wages to its recruits and hosting an army which would be defeated only at the end of the world (1 Cor. 15:26, 54–55). The rulers of this age are also hostile to the creator, having crucified Christ and made false claims for their wisdom (1 Cor. 2:6–8). Moreover, in pagan cultic feasts, demons offer food and drink to the partakers, weaning them from the table of Christ (1 Cor. 10:20–22). Both angels (which may be evil) and principalities (which include but transcend political power structures) vie for the loyalty of the believer in Jesus as the Christ (Rom. 8:38–39).

In Paul's view, therefore, the Christian lives on a battlefield. In this world of competing forces there are no fire-free zones in which the uncommitted may live; there is no arena free from the claim or dominion of some power. We see, therefore, why the term "Lord" (*Kurios*) is such a pregnant term for Paul. Informing the term is the belief that in the death and resurrection of Jesus, God has begun his final conquest of the hostile powers; the final victory is imminent when God will place all things in subjection to him (1 Cor. 15:24–25). In the meantime, the conflict between God and the hostile powers goes on. Those once held captive are now being released from the clutches of the "powers that be," but they still look forward to the final triumph of God's righteousness when Jesus' lordship will be complete.

The modern reader may find such views of personalized evil strange or even offensive. However, our memory of Nazism, and our continuing witness of racial hatred, make references to demonic forces at least not incomprehensible. And though Paul's references to apocalyptic terrors may appear to us surrealistic, we shall miss the power of individual passages, and misunderstand the letters as a whole if we cannot be sensitive to the way these mythological images informed his thought and that of his readers. Life for some was simply empty; for the others, it was absurdly oppressed—they felt helpless in the grip of forces too great for anyone to resist or even to comprehend. Paul's gospel spoke to the first of help, and to the second of salvation from their ugly web; and thus he nerved men and women for their daily lives and for the final struggle.

5. THE LAST ADAM

Richard Rubenstein, discussing Paul's use of the Adam symbol, writes, "Almost two thousand years before the depth psychology that his religious imagination helped to make possible, Paul of Tarsus gave expression to mankind's yearning for a new and flawless beginning that could finally end the cycle of anxiety, repression, desire, and craving—the inevitable con-comitants of the human pilgrimage." [8] Whatever one thinks of Rubenstein's effort to link Paul with depth psychology, his observation is correct that the Adamic myth plays a major role in Paul's thought.

Paul could have joined Hamlet in saying, "The time is out of joint." In the apostle's view, this disjointed state represents degeneration from a flawless beginning. The cosmic decline began when Adam revolted against the crea-tor's prohibition: "You shall not eat of the fruit of the tree which is in the midst of the garden, . . . lest you die." (Gen. 3:3, also 2:17) Before the cleavage man and woman lived in a state of innocence, unshamed by naked-ness, strangers to want, freely taking from nature's abundance without sweat or toil, and untroubled by anxiety over death. A friend of the animals, Adam was neither hunter nor hunted. Barely inferior to God, he shared in the crea-tion by naming the animals and he ruled the world without enmity or strife. Eve had the capacity to bear children without pain. But because of their disobedience Adam and Eve were exiled from the garden to a life marked by toil and want, fratricide and fear, and death and pain. Ever since that time mankind and nature have shared Adam's frustration and futility, and have suffered under the dominion of demonic powers. Even though Paul nowhere fully articulates this scenario, he seems to take it for granted. For although the Old Testament and the Gospels rarely mention the Adamic myth, it occupies a prominent place in Paul's letters. Three passages will receive our attention here: Romans 5:12–21; 1 Corinthians 15; and Philip-pians 2:6–11.

a. *Romans 5:12–21*

The belief was widespread in first-century rabbinic and apocalyptic thought that the original state which the world enjoyed would be restored at the end of the age. Paul obviously shared this view, but for him the agent of this restoration was the Christ whom he alternately called the "second Adam," "the last Adam," and "the Adam who is to come." In Romans 5:12–21 Paul contrasts this last Adam with the first. The two Adams were alike in that the action of each influenced the destiny of all mankind; they were different in that through the act of righteousness of the last Adam came "acquittal" for all men, whereas through the disobedience of the first Adam "many were made sinners" (Rom. 5:19). Through the last Adam came life (5:18), whereas through the first Adam came death (5:21).

Although Paul speaks of Jesus as the antitype of Adam, he is uncom-fortable with the comparison, for in Jesus, he adds, grace has abounded "much more" to mankind's good than did the sin of Adam redound to the hurt and loss of humankind. While Paul does say that sin entered the human context through Adam, he does not create or endorse the doctrine of original sin as it came to be known later. He did believe, as did every rabbi, that sin was universal and that its existence originated with Adam, but it is perpetuated through repeated acts of disobedience, not by seminal transmission. Since the beginning of time, with few exceptions (e.g., Enoch and Elijah who were sinless and therefore did not die), each person has become his or her own Adam. Paul here addresses those who wonder how it is possible for Jesus' acts of obedience and righteousness to benefit other persons. Those who comprehend what it is to be one with the first Adam, Paul argues, should have no difficulty in understanding how one can be united with the last Adam.

b. *1 Corinthians 15*

In 1 Corinthians 15 Paul answers those who are skeptical about the resurrection of the dead by appealing to the solidarity of the believer with the last Adam. Evidently it was unclear to the Corinthians how the resurrection of Jesus applied to them; his triumph over death appeared to be nothing more than the private victory of one individual. Paul argues instead that his resurrection is only the first instance of the general resurrection (1 Cor. 15:20). Jesus' rising signals the arrival of the kingdom of God and thus anticipates the imminent resurrection of those who are in him. Paul responds to those who wonder how a believer can be "in Christ" with an example that would have been familiar to any convert having the most casual acquaintance with synagogue discussions or Hebrew Scriptures:

> For as by [*dia*] a man came death,
>> by [*dia*] a man has come also the
> resurrection of the dead.
> For as in [*en*] Adam all die,
>> so also in [*en*] Christ shall all be made alive.
>
> (15:21, 22)

To be "in Adam" meant to participate in the destiny of the old Adamic humanity whereas to be "in Christ" meant to share in the power and glory of the new creation. As Robin Scroggs puts it, Christ for Paul is not just an example of but the medium through which one shares in the resurrected life.[9]

The resurrection for Paul was a bodily resurrection. In 1 Corinthians 15:35–38 Paul probably addresses Greek Christians who find the idea of a resurrection of the body crude and perhaps ridiculous. Conventional Greek piety and the major philosophical movements denigrated the importance of the body. Salvation to them meant release from, not perpetuation of, the body. In the rhetorical questions of 15:35 we may have an echo of their scorn: "How are the dead raised? With what kind of body do they come?" Paul responds first by distinguishing between different kinds of bodies—human bodies and animal bodies, fish bodies and bird bodies, and heavenly bodies and earthly bodies (15:39–40). Body for Paul was a synonym for the complete self, or all that made the self an "I." Thus, Paul here contrasts the form that the self now enjoys with the form it will take in the world to come. The form and substance which the self now has will perish, but the heavenly body will last forever (1 Cor. 15:42). Likewise, the two Adams belong to very different spheres: "The first man was from the earth, a man of dust; the second man is from heaven." (1 Cor. 15:47) This statement contrasts the first Adam—created from the ground and thus perishable— with the last Adam, who as the heavenly man is "a life-giving spirit" (15: 45). By implication both are bodies—one earthly, the other heavenly. Paul ends his somewhat tortuous, if not circular, argument with the affirmation that "Just as we have borne the image of the man of dust [Adam], we shall also bear the image of the man of heaven [Jesus]." (15:49)

c. *Philippians 2:6–11*

In Philippians 2:6–11 Paul quotes a Christian hymn in which many scholars see a contrast of Jesus with Adam. Although the hymn makes no direct mention of Adam, a contrast between Jesus and Adam seems implicit. The first strophe of the hymn refers to Jesus who "though he was in the form of God, did not count equality with God a thing to be grasped." The mention of "form" (*morphe*) evidently refers to the image of God which both Jesus and Adam (Gen. 1:26) bore. Unlike the first Adam, however, the last did not try to usurp the place of God (see Gen. 3:5), but instead took the role of a slave, becoming "obedient unto death." Where Adam sought to exalt himself, Christ humbled himself; whereas Adam rebelled against the Father, Jesus was obedient unto death. The conduct of the last Adam was a model of selflessness, obedience, innocence, and sacrifice which Paul exhorts his converts to emulate: "Let this mind be in you, which was also in Christ Jesus" (2:5, KJV). We see, therefore, that the second Adam is not only the agent of redemption, reversing the decline of the cosmos, redefining hardship and death, he is also the model of the true Adam before the fall. He retains untarnished the image of God (2 Cor. 4:4), and he will rule as Adam was meant to rule until all things are placed under him (1 Cor. 15:24–28). The last Adam serves as both the medium and the model of a restored humanity.

Our discussion of the function of myth in Paul is far from exhaustive. This treatment of representative passages aims (1) to show how, for Paul, the past was not dead nor the future unreal, and how both met and clasped hands in the present, and (2) how mythological materials grow and change. The way myth and symbol receive energetic and creative use in the letters provides a clue to certain of Paul's primary concerns. (3) Our purpose has also been to go beyond investigation of what happened ("external history") and learn how Paul and his converts experienced those happenings ("internal history"). H. Richard Niebuhr, who first used this distinction between internal and external history, writes:

To speak of history in this fashion is to try to think with poets rather than with scientists. That is what we mean, for poets think of persons, purposes and destinies. It is just their Jobs and Hamlets that are not dreamt of in philosophies which rule out from the company of true being whatever cannot be numbered or included in an impersonal pattern. . . . Hence we may call internal history dramatic and its truth dramatic truth, though drama in this case does not mean fiction.[10]

I hope that we are in agreement when I use myth where he uses drama, for through myth also we see how events are apprehended from within the community, how history is lived, and how persons interpret the way events shape their destiny. In the cult the believer was in Christ and Christ was in the believer. In the daily life of the Christian the sacrifice of Christ was reduplicated. In the attack on the demonic powers the paradise once lost was being regained.

In his ascent to the third heaven Paul was breaking the confines of this world and experiencing what defied articulation (see 2 Cor. 12:1–6). The only way to speak of it would be mythically. And since the church was frequent with such events, it had to be careful. In speaking mythically, the church constantly risked being called (and indeed becoming) a lunatic fringe interested only in subjective, individualistic experiences. It avoided that by insisting that any experience of what happened always be judged by the church's memory of what indeed did happen. Moreover, recollection had to be corporate, to weed out the faulty or the fanciful in memory. In this sense the mythological experience of the tradition is different from the private experience of a mystic and thus Paul speaks not just of his own experience of history, but of the experience he shares in and with the Christian community.

6. Currents and Crosscurrents

IN DEATH as well as in life controversy swirled around Paul. During his gentile mission heated exchanges with believers punctuated his letters. Conflict with public officials, arrest, and incarceration interrupted his ministry. Harassment and beatings at the hands of his synagogue critics sapped his energies and grieved his spirit. But even after his mission was cut short by death, Paul's power to provoke continued. Over a century after his burial his interpretation of the gospel still raised the hackles of some Jewish Christians. In one circle of believers he was tagged with the unflattering epithet Simon Magus, a demonic magician of some notoriety in Christian apocryphal materials.[1] More recently Paul stands accused of diverting Christianity out of its source in the teachings of Jesus and into the stagnant backwater of church dogma.[2] Even now, Paul's name is anathema to some who see him as a male chauvinist.

Although Paul has always had his detractors, he has also had his disciples. If the test of profound and seminal thinking is its ability to generate speculation, certainly Paul's thought qualifies as profound and seminal. In the first place his letters meant enough to merit their collection and preservation. The vigorous and imaginative understanding of gospel present in that collection spawned a whole family of imitations, the pseudo-Pauline letters. The writers of these pseudo-Paulines (Hebrews, 1 and 2 Timothy, Titus, etc.) were so impressed by Paul that they adopted his name to legitimate their interpretations. Paul's shadow also falls across various types of noncanonical Christian writings in later centuries. Among these extra-Biblical materials we find the Acts of Paul, an apocalypse of Paul, and more pseudo-Pauline letters (Hennecke, II, 133ff., 322ff., and 755ff.). Allusions to Paul and quotations from his letters abound in writings of the early church. Pivotal exegetes like Augustine and Luther found in Paul the prism through which they could see the rich colors of all Scripture. We see, therefore, Paul's power to provoke and excite has continued through the centuries. In the following pages we shall sketch the high points of that dialogue with Paul. In viewing currents and crosscurrents in the history of Pauline interpretation we gain a better appreciation of the subtlety of Paul's thought and the difficulty which certain prickly passages pose for the interpreter. Although such an appreciation is no magic formula for easy mastery of these ancient documents, it is nonetheless helpful for any reader seeking accurate assessment of Paul's thought.

We shall focus on five of the issues which have dominated Pauline interpretation over the centuries. In chronological order, they are (1) Gnosticism: the problem of evil in the world, (2) Pelagianism: the problem of sin, (3) the relationship of Paul to Jesus, (4) the relationship of Paul to his background, and (5) Paul and women.

1. GNOSTICISM: THE PROBLEM OF EVIL IN THE WORLD

The feud over the proper relationship of the Christian to the world smoldered for almost a century and then erupted into blazing fury about A.D. 150. Even as early as Colossians, written before the end of the first century, an author was attacking those in the early church who scorned the world below in favor of the world above. The worship of angels (Col. 2:18), the elevation of visionary experiences, and the promise of apotheosis for those who acquire special cosmic knowledge (2:18, 20), all reflect the otherworldly preoccupation of the writer's opponents. Their special disdain for the world also manifested itself in such prohibitions as "Do not handle, Do not taste, Do not touch" (2:21). Strangely enough a wild and reckless abandon accompanied this ascetic mentality. Those condemned for treating the world with disgust were also accused of "immorality, impurity, passion, evil desire, and covetousness" (3:5). Although world denial and physical indulgence appear to us to be mutually exclusive, a peculiar form of logic held them together for the author's opponents. Rejection of the world, they believed, demonstrated one's deliverance from the world, and indulgence in the world showed one's superiority to it. In fact, some Christian Gnostics felt *obligated* to break all of the moral strictures which earthlings consider important in order to demonstrate their loyalty to another, higher order. The important thing to see, however, is that Paul's name is invoked to refute these Gnostic innovators.

Around A.D. 100, 1 and 2 Timothy and Titus were written under Paul's name. They are called the Pastoral epistles because they instruct in the performance of pastoral offices. In these epistles the authority of Paul is likewise summoned against what the author believes are dangerous interpretations of the Christian message. But in them the profile of the opponents is sharper than in Colossians. In 1 Timothy those who have "missed the mark as regards the faith" (6:21) claim knowledge (the Greek is *gnosis* from which the term "Gnosticism" is derived). These "heretics"[3] believe that through *gnosis* they have already experienced the resurrection (2 Tim. 2:8) and thus they have overcome the world. Although they are Jews (Titus 1:10) they reject the Jewish belief in the fundamental goodness of the creation (see 1 Tim. 4:4, which opposes them by vigorously insisting on the creation's goodness). Their adherence to "godless and silly myths" (1 Tim. 4:7) and their use of "endless genealogies" (1 Tim. 1:4) reflect their belief that a hierarchy of angelic mediators separated the good God from the evil world. It would appear that the Gnostics had found support in Paul's letters for their position and our author is attempting to rescue Paul from them. The writer of the Pastorals wants to show that Paul in fact repudiated the position for which the Gnostics claim his support.

Second-century Gnosticism came and almost conquered under the banner of Paul. Although Gnosticism was multifarious, the diverse expressions of the movement held certain themes and emphases in common. Gnostic sects everywhere displayed hatred for the world and things of the flesh. Their disdain for the creation spilled over onto its creator, for, they reasoned, if the earth is evil its architect must also be evil. Christian Gnosticism, therefore, often contrasted the creator God of the Old Testament with the God revealed in Christ. One was seen as the "god of the world" and, therefore, diabolical; the other was viewed as the God of the highest heaven, and therefore, gracious and good. Salvation, naturally enough, was understood as liberation from this wretched earth and rescue from corrupted flesh. According to the Gnostic myth, through some tragic failure a spark of the divine was planted in some (but not all) persons and the memory of its divine origin erased. Humankind continued in its ignorant stupor until the high God had mercy and sent Christ to remind man of his true origin. Salvation, therefore, came through knowledge (*gnosis*) but this *gnosis* was more than just intellectual awareness of the divine origin of one's true self. Knowing for the Gnostic went beyond mental recall; it meant active reunion with one's divine source through all kinds of ecstatic experience—dreams, visions, speaking in tongues, etc. In this return to the divine source, one is liberated from the bodily prison. It was hardly surprising, therefore, that the Gnostics equated this moment of liberation with the resurrection. As the Gospel of Philip says,

> Those who say that the Lord died first and then rose up are in error, for he rose up first then died. If anyone does not first attain the resurrection, he will die. (104:15–19)[4]

Moreover, since the body shared the taint of this evil world, the whole concept of the resurrection of the body was repugnant to Gnostics. Their contempt for the world was matched by preoccupation with heavenly things— divine mysteries, esoteric wisdom, manifestations of the power of the spirit, etc. As "spiritual" beings they worshiped the spiritual man, Christ, but they conveniently ignored or even cursed the earthly Jesus.

Marcion was one of the key figures in the second-century Gnostic controversy. Although he was excommunicated by the Roman Church in A.D. 144, he and his disciples dominated Syria until the beginning of the fifth century. Orthodoxy prevailed over Marcionism only after Bishop Rabbula

(411–435) managed to have Marcionite meeting places destroyed and their property transferred to the Great Church, and after the zealous bishop "gently" persuaded Marcionites to give up their "error," be "baptized," and submit to the "truth." [5]

Interestingly enough, Paul's letters formed the heart of Marcion's Bible. And none of the Old Testament books was included. It may seem strange that the Gnostics were so fond of Paul unless one notices that certain statements of Paul, isolated from their immediate and broader context, do seem to buttress Gnostic claims. In 1 Corinthians 9:26–27 Paul speaks of the body as if it were an enemy which must be beaten into submission ("I pommel my body and subdue it"). Elsewhere Paul appears to speak pejoratively of the flesh ("nothing good dwells . . . in my flesh," Rom. 7:18). In Romans 7:24 Paul begs for deliverance from "this body of death." Romans 8:23 was a crucial passage for the Gnostics. Paul says, "we ourselves, who have the first fruits of the Spirit, groan inwardly as we wait for adoption as sons, the redemption *of* our bodies," but the Gnostics read, "redemption *from* our bodies." Since they despised the body, the Gnostics could easily join Paul in saying, "flesh and blood cannot inherit the kingdom of God." (1 Cor. 15:50)

In other passages, too, the Gnostics found Paul advocating views they cherished. They were preoccupied with "spiritual things," and with divine mysteries. Paul also, they discovered, spoke of "What no eye has seen, nor ear heard, nor the heart of man conceived." (1 Cor. 2:9) Moreover, Paul boasted of a vision in which he was "caught up into Paradise . . . [and] heard things that cannot be told, which man may not utter." (2 Cor. 12:3–4) They too aspired to fly to the third heaven (or higher) to receive special visions and to taste the ambrosial food and drink.

The Gnostics also found support in Paul for the radical dualism between the world above and the world below. In 2 Corinthians 4:4 Paul says the "god of this world has blinded the minds of the unbelievers." No doubt Paul was referring to the Devil as "god of this world," but the Gnostics interpreted the passage as referring to the creator of this world, i.e., Yahweh of Genesis. They concluded from this that it was the evil God, Yahweh, who "blinded the minds" of man so that man could no longer remember his true God "beyond all change and principality."

The stubborn insistence of the Gnostics that Yahweh was the evil "god of this [evil] world" clashed with the classic Hebrew view that Yahweh was just and merciful and that his creation was good. The Jew delighted in the pride which Yahweh took in his own craftsmanship—"and God saw everything that he had made, and behold, it was very good." (Gen. 1:31) The Gnostic rejection of the Old Testament, as the revelation of a base, pretender God, in favor of certain Christian writings threatened to drive a wedge between Hebrew Scripture and Christian revelation. This threat posed in the sharpest way the question of relationship between Jewish and Christian tradition.

Early in the second century the church fathers [6] took up the cudgels against the Gnostic position. Central to their attack was the conviction that the Hebraic Scriptures and Christian writings belonged together. They denounced as a grotesque caricature the Gnostic teaching that Yahweh was wicked. They argued instead that the God of the creation and patriarchs was the same God revealed in Jesus Christ. They tirelessly maintained that there was no basis in Paul for the dualism of the Gnostics. Origen persistently objected that there was no evidence in Paul's letters to support the view that matter *per se* is evil.[7] Irenaeus, a second-century bishop of Lugdunum (modern Lyons, in France), clearly attempted to rob the Gnostics of their base of support in Paul. He knew of the Gnostic use of Paul's statement that "flesh and blood cannot inherit the kingdom of God" (1 Cor. 15:50) to bolster their dualistic position. Against them Irenaeus submitted four reasons for belief in the resurrection of the *physical* body, all of them drawn from Paul's letters.[8]

Causing the greatest difficulty for the fathers was Paul's interpretation of the Law. The Gnostics had gathered grist for their mill from such passages as Romans 3:21 where Paul seems to do away with the Law: "now the righteousness of God has been manifested apart from law. . . ." The Gnostics had read this and similar passages as evidence that Paul also rejected the Hebrew Scriptures. The fathers were justifiably puzzled by the ambiguity and shifting emphases in many of Paul's statements about the Law. Origen, for example, noted six different ways Paul used the term "Law." [9] The fathers admitted that Paul's characteristic emphasis on grace seemed to relegate Law to a subordinate place if not cancel it out altogether. But the fathers argued that while Paul does emphasize the superiority of Christ to the Law, he nevertheless gives the Law an important place in God's unfolding drama of redemption. Once the fathers demonstrated convincingly Paul's positive use of Law they overcame the most serious objection to reading him in the light of, rather than as opposed to, his Jewish tradition. Their position prevailed and in time the Gnostic threat diminished. Nevertheless, it is important for us to see that the relationship of God to the world and the church to Judaism were such burning issues, not only because those questions are important for understanding Paul, but also because they are so near the heart of the life of faith itself. Man still wrestles with the problem of how to acclaim God's new acts without at least implicitly repudiating his old ones.

2. PELAGIANISM: THE PROBLEM OF SIN

Even during the controversy between the Christian Gnostics and the Christian mainstream, other disputes were brewing over the proper interpretation of Paul. Whereas the Gnostics longed for deliverance from the evil world, other believers were preoccupied with the problem of sin and release from its burden. This concern over salvation from sin—how God can justify the unrighteous—has fascinated western theologians from the fourth century to the present.

The principal figures in this early debate were Augustine and Pelagius, both churchmen of the late fourth and early fifth centuries. We know Augustine, of course, from his *Confessions* and from a history enriched by his theological profundity and his powerful Biblical exegesis. Pelagius, however, also a great intellect and a serious Biblical exegete, also did major commentaries on Romans and the two Corinthian letters,[10] and shorter ones on all of the other letters in the Pauline corpus.

At issue between Augustine and Pelagius was the correct understanding of the nature of sin, its origin and remedy. Long before the first ink flowed from his pen against Pelagius (A.D. 412), Augustine had already described man as a "lump of sin" who could do nothing toward his own salvation.[11] Meanwhile, in Rome, Pelagius was teaching that man had the ability within himself to live a sinless life. His exegesis of Romans led Pelagius to reject the idea that sin is transmitted like a pedigree from parent to offspring. The crucial passage in the dispute was Romans 5:12 where Paul says, "therefore as sin came into the world through one man and death through sin, and so death spread to all men because all men sinned . . . ." This passage, according to the British monk, says that the transmission of sin from Adam to all mankind is not by *propagation* but by *imitation*.[12] Man is a sinner not by birth but by choice. Since Pelagius found no support in Paul for the seminal transmission of sin, he concluded that the doctrine of original sin was a false one. Moreover, he added, it was contradictory:

> If sin is natural, it is not voluntary; if it is voluntary it is not inborn. These two definitions are as mutually contrary as are necessity and (free) will.[13]

Not only did Pelagius raise questions about the Scriptural authenticity of the doctrine of original sin and the anthropology implicit in it, he also argued that such a view undermined the Christian doctrine of God. How, he asked, could a just God create man a sinner and then condemn him for sinning? How could a righteous God command man thus, "You shall be holy, for I the LORD your God am holy" (Lev. 19:2) if he had made man congenitally incapable of holiness? How could the Son of God command the believer to be "perfect as your heavenly Father is perfect" (Mt. 5:48) if man is so stained by sin at birth that he is incapable of perfection?

Pelagius was quick to see the implications of this understanding of Paul for the practise of infant baptism. Since he rejected the doctrine of original sin, he denied that babies were in need of cleansing from the stain of sin. Although he endorsed infant baptism he balked at the suggestion that it was necessary for the salvation of the child.

Seeing the position of Pelagius, it is easy to understand why he was infuriated by a line from one of Augustine's most famous prayers which reads: "Grant what You command, and command what You will." [14] Such an attitude, Pelagius argued, undermined genuine moral striving and sanctioned the moral indifference which he saw on every side in Rome.[15] Now that it had become socially acceptable to become a Christian, Pelagius feared the gradual reduction of the high ethical imperative in Paul's gospel to the prevailing cultural low.

It was not long before Pelagius and Augustine collided. In A.D. 412 Augustine began writing to expose the errors of his rival. He attacked both Pelagius' understanding of sin and his doctrine of man. He disputed Pelagius' claim that God, not man, should be blamed for the existence of sin if human nature is sinful from birth. On the contrary, Augustine objected, God made Adam and Eve free and innocent. It was through their rebellion, not by God's design, that man became a sinner. Adam was able to introduce sin into the human context, but he was unable to remove it. It was inconceivable to Augustine that Adam the sinner could produce innocent offspring. Consequently, in his view the whole human experiment begun by God was blighted by Adam's fatal error.

Augustine believed that Romans 5:12 supported his understanding of sin. Working out of a Latin text he read *in quo* as masculine even though *quo* could be read as neuter, changing the meaning entirely. Augustine understood Romans 5:12 to say that "death came to all men, *in whom* (*in quo*, i.e., Adam) all men sinned." Thus he assumed that he was faithfully transmitting the Pauline view. The Greek text, however, requires reading the Latin *in quo* as neuter thus giving, "death came to all men, *because* all men sinned." Paul obviously is indebted to the Jewish tradition that holds that each person becomes his own Adam by choice ("because"), not by inheritance. The apostle did hold that social context put strong pressure on man to act selfishly, but he hardly held the view of "original sin" as we know it.

Augustine further argued that Pelagius not only underestimated the power of sin, but he also overestimated man's power to cope with it. For once Adam introduced sin into the human framework the trap was sprung. Man could neither remove it from the world nor eradicate it from his own nature. Since man was powerless to help himself, his salvation had to come from a source outside his world. This remedy is provided as a gracious act of God through Jesus Christ. Infants need baptism, Augustine contended, because from the very beginning they need redemption from the sin of Adam. To those who objected that such redemption could be effected only by faith, and therefore it was not available to untutored infants, Augustine retorted that faith is not a human work but a gracious gift of the Father. For his salvation man is totally dependent on God and there is nothing he can do to effect his own redemption.

The charge by Pelagius that total reliance on God sanctioned moral indifference brought an angry reply from Augustine. Like the ancient rabbis he placed statements about God's grace and human responsibility side by side without sensing any tension between them. Pelagius saw the Christian life as a cooperative affair; one half of the responsibility belongs to God who gives man the *ability* to do right; the other half of the responsibility belongs to man who exercises that ability. Appealing to Paul, Augustine on the other hand viewed the work of divine grace and human response in paradoxical and total terms; all is given by God, yet all is required of man.

In the opinion of Augustine, Pelagius' confidence in human achievement took the power to direct history out of the hands of God and placed it in the hands of man. For if man is the maker of his own destiny and has the ability to direct the course of history, the doctrine of the sovereignty of God is needless, or worse. Pelagius' emphasis on human freedom and responsibility virtually eclipsed the traditional stress on divine providence. Augustine, on the other side, resorted to the use of the paradox once again to hold the two motifs in balance. Drawing on Paul's discussion of predestination in Romans 9:14ff., he coupled opposing statements in an attempt to state a profound truth: All things are predestined by God; man is totally free and responsible.

The debate between Pelagius and Augustine raged for six years. Finally, in 418 Pelagius was officially condemned by the Synod of Carthage and dropped out of sight. The debate continued, however, in spite of the official condemnation because "it was a real debate on central issues of Christian faith." [16] Over a thousand years later Martin Luther felt that the anti-Pelagian tracts of Augustine still addressed the most urgent question of his time. Augustine and Luther clearly are brothers in their assessment of the depravity of man and the grace of God. Both came to their understanding of the gospel after searing personal struggles, and both found their way out of their distress through Paul's letters. It is not surprising that Luther, with his history of personal struggle, should regard as nonsense Pelagius' belief that man can keep God's commandments. With great poignancy Luther describes his collision with Romans 1:17 and its obstinate refusal to surrender its meaning. He was galled by Paul's statement that "the *justice* of God is being revealed from heaven against all ungodliness and wickedness" (trans. mine), and he was angry at God for exacting justice even through his gospel. For no matter how hard Luther tried he still failed to fulfill God's just demand. If salvation depends on performing the impossible, how could man ever be saved? Near despair Luther noticed the context of Romans 1:17. With astonishment he read the words, "the just shall live by faith." (KJV) He was relieved to learn that it was through faith not works that man was placed in a proper relationship with God. This emphasis on God's justification of the sinner held enormous implications for the interpretation of Scripture and gave the interpretation of Paul a critical significance in the theological debates which followed. In assessing these men and the implications of their thought for our understanding of Paul, we should remember that Pelagius was, as well as Augustine or Luther, a committed Christian eager to discern and propagate the faith. He raised questions about troublesome passages which we cannot avoid in a close reading of Paul's letters. Augustine misreads Romans 5:17 (see above) but Pelagius fails to appreciate fully either the power or mystery of human sin. So which is more faithful to Paul? Whether they realize it or not most American Protestants come to the letters with spectacles provided either by Luther or Augustine. For justification by faith which was central to the thought of both men has traditionally assumed a dominant place in American Protestantism. No doubt the motif *is* critical to Paul's argument in Romans and Galatians. But it is mentioned infrequently or not at all in the other letters. We shall need to be careful in reading these other letters lest our preoccupation with the guilt of the individual and God's grace blind us to the great variety and scope of Paul's concern. Some scholars feel that Paul's thought should be viewed in a broader cosmic frame which includes but transcends the emphasis on individual salvation. Others argue that justification by faith is the center of gravity of the whole body of Pauline letters. It is these unresolved issues that continue to make the reading of Paul an exciting and challenging experience for inquiring minds.

3. THE RELATIONSHIP OF PAUL AND JESUS

"Jesus was not a Christian, he was a Jew." So spoke Wellhausen in 1905. Many would still heartily agree. They image Jesus as a charismatic Galilean who had uncanny feel for the essence of true religion. Trusting completely in God he lived a life free of anxiety and devoid of pretense. He cared little for religious rules or rituals, and he stepped across social barriers to befriend criminals, prostitutes, the poor, and little children. But somehow the primitive and beautiful religion of this Jewish peasant has been spoiled by the professionals, obscured by theological overlay, cluttered by dogmatic assertion, and robbed of vitality by an institutional form. Usually in this scenario it is Paul who is called the initial corrupter of a vital, true religion. According to this view, Paul's insistence on the Jesus of the cross totally eclipsed Jesus the teacher in parables. Paul pushed aside the "gentle Jesus meek and mild" in favor of the vindictive judge coming with God's angels in flaming fire. He forced Jesus' simple announcement "your sins are forgiven" (Mk. 2:5) to give way to theological speculation about guilt and redemption. This interpretation holds that the history of Christianity would have been entirely different had Paul influenced only a small circle of disciples. Paul's interpretation was decisive, however, because his influence was so far-flung. As the Johnny Appleseed of early Christianity he planted the seeds of the gospel from Antioch to Rome. As the founder of churches he locked the religion of

Jesus in an institutional case. It was Paul, many feel, who cut Christianity off from its roots in the life and teachings of Jesus, the Galilean holy man.

This contemporary juxtaposition of Jesus and Paul has a long history. As early as the seventeenth century, John Locke, an English Deist, saw such a cleavage. He reached this conclusion after beginning a search for a "reasonable Christianity" free from the "shackles of dogma." He wanted to make a fresh appraisal of the New Testament independent of the bias of a Christian orthodoxy. This independent study convinced him that a great chasm ran through the New Testament between the simple gospel of Jesus and the complicated, obscure theology of Paul. The gospel *of* Jesus, according to Locke, came from the lips of Jesus himself, but the gospel *about* Jesus was the invention of later interpreters like Paul. The implications of Locke's study were clear. If one is to recover the message of Jesus in its pristine purity, one must strip off all dogmatic distortions whether of the Church of England or of the apostle Paul himself. It is the four Gospels which must be used as the primary and even exclusive source if the simple gospel of Jesus is to be reclaimed.

This tendency to divorce the teaching of Jesus from the theology of Paul reached its apogee in the thought of William Wrede (1859–1906), a brilliant German Biblical scholar. In his view, Jesus was a simple, pious Jewish peasant whose prophetic insight, moral sensitivity, empathy for the oppressed, and strong sense of the presence of God meant nothing to Paul. Although Jesus was remembered by the apostle as a real historical figure, the particulars of his earthly life meant little to Paul. Before Paul came, Wrede argued, Christianity was only "an inner Jewish sect," but after Paul we have "a Christian Church." [17] According to Wrede, the religion of Jesus is true Christianity, but the religion of Paul is a fabricated and institutionalized dogma.

Very recently Géza Vermès, an Oxford Reader in Jewish Studies, has tried once again to untangle the Jesus of history from the Christ of dogma, in his *Jesus the Jew* (London: Collins, 1973). Vermès' study of the Dead Sea Scrolls and Talmud persuades him that Jesus is fully understandable only within the framework of first-century Judaism in Galilee. He finds in northern Palestine strong interest in the Elijah miracle tradition and in meditation, which would explain Jesus' acceptance there, and his mixed reception in Jerusalem. Presumably religious enthusiasm and ignorance of rabbinic tradition were viewed differently in Galilee and in Jerusalem. Placing Jesus in this Galilean setting, Vermès contends that Jesus probably did not claim to be the messiah, that he certainly did not claim to be divine, and that he would have been outraged by the incarnation formula "very God of very God, very man of very man." Vermès believes that it was Hellenistic paganism, not Paul, which led gentile Christianity into error; nevertheless, it was church doctrine that spoiled the simple religion of this pious Galilean peasant and his Jewish followers. It is hard to understand why Paul should escape the blame since he enjoyed the greatest success in interpreting Christian gospel for the Hellenistic mind. Vermès' approach avoids some of the mistakes of the earlier scholars, but the jury is still out on his case. It would seem, however, that the challenge his thesis poses has already been met by two earlier developments in this century: (1) the advent of form criticism and (2) the studies of Albert Schweitzer.

Rudolf Bultmann and Martin Dibelius first taught us that the traditions of Jesus circulated orally in certain forms (parables, sayings, miracle stories, etc.) long before they were assembled and edited by the Gospel writers. Through his careful study of the forms, Bultmann was able to show that the church not only kept alive the Jesus materials by oral tradition, it also shaped and interpreted them to fit the changing needs of the church. Gradually it also became evident that the Gospel writers further shaped, edited, and interpreted the materials which they got from the oral stream, in order to speak to their own times. Scholars now realize that the Gospel writers were not composing objective biographies of Jesus, but were writing their story of Jesus' life with a strong theological emphasis. Mark, for example, underscores the importance of Jesus as the suffering Son of God. Matthew emphasizes Jesus' role as the eschatological teacher. Luke speaks of Jesus as the bearer of the Holy Spirit, the friend of the poor, and the fulfillment of Israel's hopes. Through form criticism we have learned to appreciate the Gospel writers as creative authors who left their imprint on their work through their selection, arrangement, and interpretation of the oral tradition. Once it is realized that the Gospel writers as well as Paul had strong theological interests, the old view that the Jesus of the Gospels was free of dogmatic interpretation is no longer defensible. If any transformation had taken place, it clearly was not the work of Paul alone.

When Albert Schweitzer died in 1965 he was eulogized as one of the great human beings of our century, and he was. As a missionary doctor in French Equatorial Africa, an accomplished musician, the winner of the Nobel Peace Prize, and an Alsatian writer, he had captured the imagination of the western world. But it was his Biblical scholarship which led him in the first place to give up promising careers in music, theology, and philosophy to found the hospital in Africa. When Schweitzer went to Africa in 1913 he carried with him the rough copy of his book on Paul. Fifteen years later Schweitzer found time to prepare that manuscript for publication. When his book, *The Mysticism of Paul the Apostle,* did appear, it was revolutionary. Even today scholars consider acquaintance with Schweitzer's work to be an absolute requirement for discussion of Jesus and Paul. In 1906 Schweitzer had found his clue for understanding Jesus in Jewish apocalyptic thought. Now he argued that Paul, likewise, understood Jesus in light of Jewish apocalypticism. In the first century, the view was commonplace in Jewish circles that

God's eschatological rule would be ushered in by a period of intense suffering. Jesus, Schweitzer argued, identified his own rejection and death with the final trauma that would bring in God's rule. Paul likewise saw the cross as the pain accompanying the birth of the new age. Schweitzer concluded from this that in their common reliance on Jewish apocalyptic and in their understanding of the passion Paul and Jesus were in perfect agreement.

Some scholars correctly note flaws in Schweitzer's work.[18] Others even accuse him of making ground-level mistakes. His view that Jesus deliberately courted death to hasten God's final denouement is nowhere accepted, and the mystical solidarity with Christ effected in baptism is hardly the essence of Paul's thought. But all would agree that Schweitzer opened up new dimensions and raised profound questions concerning the relationship of Paul and Jesus. Whatever faults Schweitzer's work may have, there is no escaping his essential point—that both the character of Jesus' life and ministry and the proclamation of Paul were eschatological through and through, and both must be assessed in the full light of Jewish apocalyptic thought. Unquestionably, however, Paul's letters differ from the Gospels in style and emphasis. Long involved discussions weave complicated patterns in the epistles. Short, pithy sayings dart from the lips of Jesus. Paul's letters are heavy with abstractions (e.g., the righteousness of God). Authentic Jesus materials such as the parables bear the unmistakable aroma of this earth. Paul's frequent allusions to the *parousia* (the second coming of Christ) would sound unnatural on Jesus' lips. The postresurrection situation and Paul's worldwide mission summon forth themes in Paul that were muted or absent in Jesus' ministry. Paul has reflected long and deeply on the meaning of the Christ event. But, even though Paul has modified the traditions and created new centers of meaning in Christian thought, his theology does not contradict the proclamation of Jesus. His work is an extension and even a reformulation of the meaning of the Christ event but he and Jesus are no more incompatible than are Bartok and Beethoven.

4. THE RELATIONSHIP OF PAUL TO HIS BACKGROUND

Paul's theology is often portrayed as the antithesis not only of the teachings of Jesus, but also, paradoxically enough, of first-century Judaism. When Paul entered the Christian church it is assumed that he repudiated his Jewish past, recalling it only in order to throw his Christian status into bold relief. In the conversion experienced by Augustine, Luther, and the Pietists, it is generally believed, we have a carbon copy of Paul's own spiritual biography.

"Pick it up, read it; pick it up, read it," Augustine heard a child singing. So he took up the Bible before him and his eyes singled out Romans 13:13, "not in reveling and drunkenness, not in debauchery and licentiousness, not in quarreling and jealousy. But put on the Lord Jesus Christ, and make no provision for the flesh, to gratify its desires." Augustine reported that, instantly, as the sentence ended, there was infused in my heart something like the light of full certainty and all of the gloom of doubt vanished away.[19]

So ended Augustine's long, dark night of the soul. His experiments with philosophy and Manicheanism had left him empty and restless. His excursion into hedonism was unsatisfying. But with his conversion to Christianity Augustine felt that his period of blind groping had ended. The change in Augustine was dramatic. In a sensitive discussion of his pilgrimage of faith, he contrasted the dissatisfaction and aimless searching before his conversion with the peace and purpose he felt after baptism. Even the birds knew, he said, that he was a Christian.

In many ways Luther's experience paralleled that of Augustine. Restless and dissatisfied Luther left the study of law at the university hoping to find peace in a monastery. But despite herculean efforts to live a blameless life, he felt condemned, empty and wanting. Release came for this troubled, uneasy monk through his discovery of Paul's emphasis on salvation by grace alone. A total reorientation in his self-understanding and theological outlook occurred. Energies once sapped by anxiety and guilt burst forth anew in highly creative ways.

The Pietists of the late sixteenth and seventeenth centuries likewise found support in Paul for a strong emphasis on conversion. In Romans 7 and 8 they thought they found evidence that Paul divided life into two stages, one falling before, the other after conversion. They read the first person singular references in Romans 7 as autobiographical statements which Paul made about his life as an unconverted, frustrated, guilt-ridden Pharisee. They pointed to verse 9 where Paul says, "I was once alive apart from the law, but when the commandment came, sin revived and I died." In verse 15 they witnessed Paul distracted, utterly confused: "I do not understand my own actions. For I do not do what I want, but I do the very thing I hate." This inward struggle, they believed, finally erupted in a cry of defeat, in verse 24: "Wretched man that I am! Who will deliver me from this body of death?"

In the view of the Pietists, chapter 8, on the other hand, speaks of Paul's Christian life after conversion. After the light of Christ had illumined his night, Paul can speak triumphantly: "Who shall separate us from the love of Christ? Shall tribulation, or distress, or persecution, or famine, or nakedness, or peril, or sword? . . . No, in all these things we are more than conquerors through him who loved us." (vss. 35, 37) The Pietist warmth over Paul's conversion was further supported by an appeal to his Damascus Road experience (Acts 9:1–9; 22:6–11; 26:12–18). Upon conversion Paul, the zealous Pharisee, finally acknowledged that his efforts to keep the Law had failed. Now he openly admitted what he had tried to conceal by frenetic activity. Now the ethical crisis was overcome in a dramatic conversion by which he found release from enormous psychological tension.

The numerator in the experiences of Augustine, Luther, and the Pietists was in each case different, but the denominator was the same. All spoke poignantly of their rescue from a dreadful past. All viewed their life under grace as the exact reverse of their former life. And all found in the letters of Paul the inspiration and direction for their metamorphosis. Given the pattern of their experience it was natural for them to see in Paul the same rupture as theirs between the way of unbelief and the life of faith. Paul the Jew was called the unbeliever; Paul the emissary of Christ was made the model of faith. Paul the devotee of Law was cast as a wayward, guilt-ridden Pharisee; Paul the recipient of grace became the apostle of freedom. Understandably such an assessment of Paul tended to drive a wedge between his existence in Christ and his Jewish life under the Law.

Without question, the idea that Jesus was the messiah was flatly rejected by most Jews. Paul himself ran into conflict with the synagogue, and he dismisses as "dung" his considerable achievements under the Law (*skubalon*, Phil. 3:8). He speaks with remorse of his persecution of the church before he reversed himself to become its foremost advocate. And finally, he speaks movingly of the revelation of God's righteousness "apart from Law" (Rom. 3:21). All of this seems to argue a radical discontinuity between Paul the Christian and Paul the Jew.

A growing number of scholars, however, question this interpretation. They point out that Paul nowhere suggests either that he found the Law intolerable or that he felt conscience-stricken because his feverish attempts to keep it had failed. On the contrary, in Philippians 3:6 Paul says he was "under the law blameless." Even Romans 8:2 should not be read to mean that the two eras are incompatible. There he mentions two laws: "the law of the Spirit of life in Christ Jesus has set me free from the law of sin and death." Whatever life in the Spirit was for Paul, it was not lawlessness. Was Paul here, like Jeremiah, suggesting that the gap between God's requirement (Mosaic Law) and man's response had been overcome? If so, he may not be repudiating the Law but rather announcing the day of the Lord when the gulf which existed in Torah between God's speaking and man's hearing was overcome. Jeremiah heard God say, "I will put my law within them, and I will write it upon their hearts." Jeremiah did not mean that God's Torah would be repudiated, but that human resistance to the divine will would end. Evidently Paul believed that the time had arrived: God would etch his law of the Spirit on the human heart, and man's stubbornness before God's will would vanish.

It is also misleading if not erroneous to suggest that Paul rejected his past when he became an apostle. Paul often speaks positively of his Jewish past (Rom. 9:4–5). And very often he speaks of the coming of the Messiah as the fulfillment of God's promise to the Jews. He quotes from the prophets who anticipated God's new day in Jesus, and he believes that salvation not only emerged from the Jews, but will also embrace them at the end of history (Rom. 11).

In addition, Paul's eschatology closely resembles that found in Jewish apocalyptic literature. In his eager waiting for God's final visitation as well as in the way he pictures the end, Paul is at one with much of first-century Judaism. The difference between them is found in Paul's belief that the end was already beginning—had been begun by Jesus. According to Jewish apocalypticism God's cosmic clock read five minutes before midnight; for Paul the first bong of the midnight hour had sounded. We see, therefore, that although there were differences between the views of Paul and those of his Jewish contemporaries, the distinction was not total. Even Paul's reference to his achievements under the Law as "refuse" (Phil. 3:8) was not a repudiation of his past but a revaluation of that past in light of his participation in the new age of Christ.

Almost daily we are made painfully aware of the separation of Judaism and Christianity. History books are replete with bitter and shameful strife between Jews and Christians. Synagogue members go to their worship on Friday night and Saturday; Christians gather on Sunday. Time and again ugly acts of anti-Semitism have stained the hands of man and aggravated the old divisions. All of our history and much of our present experience underscores the difference between these sister faiths. We should be careful, however, when we project patterns we take for granted back on the time of Paul. Nowhere does Paul speak of Christianity as an entity separate from Judaism. Everywhere he envisions his gentile mission as a part of God's promise to Israel to include all nations in his final redeemed human family. As we read the letters of Paul, therefore, let us guard against the too-common assumption that Paul rejected the tradition he once loved.

Not only does this dislocation of Paul from his background do violence to his thought, but it also distorts our picture of first-century Jewish faith. A rather poor likeness of first-century Judaism has often been drawn by merely reversing everything Paul says about his life in Christ. Paul's gospel was joyful so Judaism is depicted as joyless. Paul felt free from sin and death through grace; Jews, so it was said, were yoked by the Law to sin, by sin to death. The God of Paul appears as a God of grace; the God of the Jews is cast as a severe taskmaster. Paul was self-giving; the Jews were self-seeking. As official warders of the Law, the Jews became insufferable religious snobs. If they kept the Law's letter they ignored its spirit, and were self-righteous hypocrites. And if they did not keep its letter they were engulfed in a fog of guilt and anxiety. The more we know about first-century Judaism the better we realize that the reconstruction above is an absurd parody. Through the scrolls left from the Qumran community near the Dead Sea we have gained a better understanding of both the variety and the nature of first-century Hebraic life and thought. The community attended to God's

Law, but it knew itself also as the beneficiary of God's grace. One faithful member says, "if I stagger, God's mercies are my salvation forever; and if I stumble because of the sin of the flesh, my justification is in the righteousness of God" (from "The Scroll of the Rule," XI:12).[20] The community opposed insincerity and hypocrisy. Their piety, moreover, although intense was hardly joyless. We see, therefore, that the Judaism invoked to show Paul to greatest advantage bears little resemblance to the Judaism that was.

Reading Paul by the light of the total reversals in Luther and Augustine at their conversion not only sets Paul adrift from his moorings in Judaism, but it also tends to focus our attention too narrowly on the salvation of the individual. With our attention riveted to this motif, as important as it is, we sometimes neglect other emphases in the letters. Most scholars would readily agree that Paul's theology is multi-dimensional. Disagreement exists, however, about what is the prevailing motif in that theology. Scholarly opinion has fluctuated from the view that Paul's message was individualistic to the core, to the belief his gospel was communal throughout. One focuses on the individual; the other encompasses the whole range of salvation history. Perhaps the works of Rudolf Bultmann and Johannes Munck best pose these alternatives for us.

Rudolf Bultmann, possibly the most influential Biblical scholar of our century, found the key to Paul's theology in his understanding of man.[21] In formulating Paul's anthropology, Bultmann relies for his insight and categories mainly on existentialist thought. Paul was aware, he believed, of the one question which forces itself on all humanity: Can a person be open to the future which stretches out before him? Each person yearns to be free enough to be open and honest in each encounter. In spite of this longing for truth in the inward being, however, each person feels that his life lacks the integrity, authenticity, and fulfillment which belong to his true nature. Man begins, therefore, with a deep sense of loss. Each man wants authentic existence; but each refuses to believe that such comes only as a gift from God —as a reprieve from self. Each tries to secure authentic life by his efforts, not realizing that self-assertiveness always ends in self-detection and doubt.

The self-reliant spirit manifests itself in many ways, religious as well as secular. To attain to oneness with the cosmos, some perform sedulous religious duties—only to become self-righteous, and thus divided from all things. Others labor for recognition, cash, authority, children—only to find that in truth they are working solely against the suspicion of personal inadequacy. Man's best efforts fail to secure what man wants, precisely because they are efforts—premeditated and self-conscious. The authentic existence he searches for is as elusive as the end of a rainbow. Yet he is also unable to accept life from God because God is out of his control. To enjoy freedom he would have to surrender autonomy and he finds that risk too great. Fear and anxiety attend this fruitless search. The more insecure he is the more he turns in on himself; the more he turns in on himself the more insecure he is. Man is trapped, unable to break out of this vicious circle.

This tangled web over man is cut only through the proclamation of the word of God—or rather the question of God. God's grace comes to man, but not to support man's efforts at regularizing the future; God's grace comes as a question: "Will you surrender, utterly surrender, to God's dealing?" [22] Through the acceptance of grace, man rests secure in the knowledge that he is loved. Thus he is released from his self-preoccupation to be open to the future. Now man is free; risk is possible; anxiety is overcome. But this authentic existence is not realized once and for all; it must be continually re-presented in the question of God and the renewed acceptance by man.

It is clear from this summary that Bultmann sees salvation for the individual as the governing theme of Paul's theology. Understandably, therefore, Bultmann takes scant notice of the broad historical themes in Paul's letters (e.g., Rom. 9–11). For this brilliant scholar, decisive history is not world history, but the experience of each person.

Against Bultmann's understanding of Paul stands the work of Johannes Munck, *Paul and the Salvation of Mankind* (Richmond: John Knox Press, 1959). The book opens with a study of Paul's Damascus Road experience. In the traditional view, that experience is seen as a release from pent-up frustrations accumulated through Paul's repeated, unsuccessful attempts to keep the Law, and from guilt heaped up by his compulsive hatred and fanatical persecution of innocent Christians. Like a boil opening to release its poison, so this theory goes, through the conversion Paul's life was cleansed of its gangrenous infection. Munck objects that neither in Acts nor in Paul's own letters is there a hint that Paul's pre-conversion history groaned under any such heavy psychological burden. Instead, Munck argues, Paul's Damascus experience conforms rather closely to the pattern of Old Testament prophetic calls. Paul, like Jeremiah and Isaiah, says that God "set me apart before I was born" (Gal. 1:15, see also Rom. 1:1; Jer. 1:5; Is. 49:1). In Galatians 1:15–16, as also in Isaiah and Jeremiah, the call "from the womb" was linked with the mission to the gentiles. Just as the prophets served under constraint, so Paul was under compulsion to fulfill Christ's commission. According to Munck, these similarities place Paul among the ranks of the prophets. And like those prophets, he had a peculiar role to play in the history of God's people. Unlike the Old Testament prophets, however, Paul's role was to be acted out during the final scene in God's historical drama. In fact, as *the* apostle to the gentiles Paul was assigned the lead role before the curtain was to fall. The end of the age was delayed, Paul believed, so that the gentiles could be brought into the community of God's people. In other words, the end of the world stood waiting for the completion of Paul's mission.

Romans 9–11 assumes pivotal significance for Munck's thesis. In traditional Jewry the question was often asked, "what is holding back the coming of the messiah?" The usual answer was that only when Israel is converted can the messianic age come. Paul's mission to the gentiles enunciated in Romans 9–11, therefore, becomes essential for the success of God's plan. The strategy was to use the conversion of the gentiles to arouse jealousy in the Jews and thus lead them to salvation. Paul's conviction that his role was crucial for the redemption of all mankind informed everything he did.

Even the offering which Paul collected for the "poor among the saints" in Jerusalem Munck fits neatly into this scheme. This act, like the prophetic signs of old, was pregnant with meaning. From Old Testament prophecy, Israel expected that in the messianic age gentiles would stream to Jerusalem bearing tribute. Therefore when Paul, along with a delegation from the gentile churches, brought the offering up to Jerusalem, the act took on powerful eschatological significance. It was designed to announce the arrival of the messianic age to all Jews.

In this brief resumé of Munck's thesis we have passed over many stimulating features of his work. Even this short summary, however, shows where he and Bultmann differ. Where for Bultmann the dominant theme in Paul is the salvation of the individual, for Munck everything in Paul is subordinated to the eschatological mission. The purpose of this mission was not the conversion of the individual but the reassertion of God's domain over his entire creation. Whatever the blemishes of his work (and there are many),[23] Munck has at least taught us the hazard of melting Paul's thought down into a single element—the singular preoccupation with the individual and his salvation.[24] Perhaps a swing to the opposite extreme is equally unwise. Paul is concerned for the salvation of the individual (1 Cor. 5:5) but never in isolation from wider historical and corporate concerns. Paul's theology does bracket themes as large as the cosmos itself (Rom. 8:19ff.), but the individual is not thereby reduced to the status of an insect. Given our emphasis on the gospel as a resource for the "inner life," and given our tendency to view matters of faith as private affairs, it is no accident that we look for the individual emphasis in most things we read. I do not wish to speak against the dignity or worth of the individual, but it must be said that such an emphasis if taken alone stands in real tension with the outlook of Paul. God's call, for Paul, is more than a summons to enjoy salvation; it is an invitation to participate in a divine happening that is bigger than oneself—God's salvation of the entire world—human and nonhuman. It is well to remember that for the apostle there was simply no separation between individual fulfillment and group participation. To be in the community of God's people was in and of itself fulfillment on the highest level. So although in a certain sense Paul's message was personal, it was never private.

5. PAUL AND WOMEN

Paul, according to George Bernard Shaw, is "the eternal enemy of Woman." [25] In Shaw's view, Paul insisted that the wife "should be rather a slave than a partner, her real function being, not to engage a man's love and loyalty, but on the contrary to release them for God by relieving the man of all preoccupation with sex just as in her capacity of housekeeper and cook she relieves his preoccupation with hunger. . . ." [26] The prevailing popular view of Paul suggests that his view of woman was, to say the least, patronizing. For even while urging mutual love and respect between husband and wife, he commanded the woman to be submissive to her husband (Eph. 5:22ff.) and he officially endorsed the subordination of women by forbidding them to exercise authority over men (1 Tim. 2:12). Women are to fulfill the divine purpose by having children (1 Tim. 2:15). And did not Paul relegate women to a second-class citizenship when he called on them to be silent in the churches (1 Cor. 14:34)? Paul's own decision for celibacy, and his admonition to others to follow his example (1 Cor. 7:7), lend credibility to this unflattering picture.

In 1972 Professor Robin Scroggs, a respected Pauline scholar, issued a caveat against this popular caricature.[27] He correctly noted that the primary support for the view of Paul as a male chauvinist comes from pseudo-Pauline materials (1 & 2 Timothy, Ephesians, and Colossians). He joined other scholars in arguing that 1 Corinthians 14:33b–36 ("women should keep silence in the churches") was inserted by a later hand to bring 1 Corinthians into conformity with the outlook of the pseudo-Paulines.[28] Indeed, Paul assumes elsewhere that women are to be vocal participants in church (1 Cor. 11:5). Moreover, as Scroggs is aware, 1 Corinthians 7:1 ("It is well for a man not to touch a woman") was probably not Paul's view but a slogan of the Corinthian church.[29] And even if it was Paul's view, it expresses his response to an emergency rather than his disdain for women. It was common in Jewish circles to suspend normal activities in times of great crisis (e.g., during holy war men gave up not only sex but also business dealings).

First Corinthians 11:2–16 poses more of a problem, however. There Paul seems to locate woman in an inferior position in the hierarchy of creation. God is the head of Christ, Christ is the head of man, man is the head of woman. Taking for granted that Christ was pre-existent and therefore active in the creation of the world, Paul speaks of him as the head (i.e., source) of man even as man was the source of woman (via the rib). Scroggs argues that Paul is here concerned with *origins,* not with superiority or inferiority. And Paul stresses different origins, says Scroggs, to show that it has been God's plan since the creation to keep men and women distinct, and that distinction must be maintained. In other words, the apostle is responding to what he judges as a scandalous view—that in Christ *all* distinctions disappear, even those between male and female.

Scroggs concludes that there is no substance to the charge that Paul was an "eternal enemy" of women. On the contrary, he finds support in the letters for an enlightened or even liberationist view. Scroggs argues that Paul "proclaimed the complete equality within the community of all people and groups. *Distinctions* between groups remain. *Values* and *roles* built upon such distinctions are destroyed. Every human being is equal before God in Christ and thus before each other."[30] Scroggs also notes that Paul lists women among his co-workers and alludes to a number of women who are active (presumably as leaders) in the church.[31]

Many scholars are delighted that Professor Scroggs was willing to step forward and challenge the popular and persistent notion of Paul's view of women. Few would quarrel with either the spirit or substance of his defense, for Paul is nowhere overtly hostile to women. Nevertheless, Scroggs' argument that Paul was a women's liberationist has raised some eyebrows.

Recently, Professor Elaine Pagels has expressed reservations about Scroggs' argument.[32] Although Paul can say that slaves are free men in Christ, he quite obviously does not challenge the institution of slavery.[33] In a similar way, Paul's affirmation that women are equal does not mean he is challenging "the social structures that perpetuate their present subordination."[34] Professor Pagels remains unconvinced by Scroggs' interpretation of 1 Corinthians 11:2–16, an admittedly difficult passage. In his statement that Christ is the source of man and man the source of woman, Paul does seem to fall back on the natural order to argue for the subordination of women.[35] Especially troublesome is Paul's statement in 11:7 that man is the glory of God while woman is the glory of man. Pagels believes Paul views "certain incidents or practices in the Corinthian community—provoked by the presence of unveiled women believers—to be disorderly or even scandalous,"[36] and that by appealing to the primeval—i.e., divine—order, he hopes to restrict women's activity and thus restore order. Professor Pagels does not mention Paul's corrections of male conduct—these would seem to make men also responsible for the restoration of order (11:4, 7).

As the scholarly debate over Paul's view of women continues, much remains unresolved. But the discussion has produced some positive fruit. The conventional picture of Paul as a culture-bound male chauvinist has collapsed under close investigation. In many ways Paul's views contradict those of his Jewish background. He plainly expects that women will take an active role in the worship and witness of the church. Moreover, the even-handed way that Paul addresses both men *and* women in 1 Corinthians 7 is instructive. This equal share of responsibility apportioned to each suggests at least approximate equality in the partnership. That in itself is somewhat revolutionary. And Professor David Daube has shown that Paul's expectation that a woman (in Christ) could consecrate her marriage with an unbelieving husband has no Jewish precedent (see 1 Cor. 7:14).[37] According to Jewish tradition it was the male and only the male who consecrated the marriage. However murky 1 Corinthians 11:2–16 may appear, it seems clear that Paul lays a heavy burden on male *and* female to preserve the order of the church. Some degree of subordination of woman, however, may be taken for granted (especially in 11:7), but it is often overlooked that Paul's main point is the distinction between the sexes not the dominance of one over the other.

In any case Scroggs and Pagels would agree that it is unfair to criticize Paul for not challenging the structures of discrimination against women. While it is true Paul's gospel makes many structures seem unjust, it does not overtly call for their abolition. We cannot conclude from this that Paul either did or did not approve of such social practices. Paul may simply have found it unnecessary to challenge authoritarian structures, because he thought they would soon be gone. In 1 Corinthians 7:31 he expressly encourages his readers to "deal with the world as though they had no dealings with it. For the form of this world is passing away."

It is likely that Paul was neither a chauvinist nor a liberationist but something in between. The evidence is contradictory. One cannot dismiss Paul's evenhanded treatment of men and women, his references to women as his co-workers, or his assumption that women would actively participate in church worship. At the same time, some degree of subordination seems to be taken for granted in Paul's statement that man is "the image and glory of God; but woman is the glory of man" (1 Cor. 11:7). It would be remarkable indeed if Paul did not reflect some of the prejudice, superstition and bias of his own time. The question is, how much should we worry about Paul's cultural views? Does his unconsidered prejudice against women vitiate his views on Jesus, and on other important questions of life? Theologians have long argued that the gospel is greater than any particular witness to it. (Perhaps that is why we retain the versions of Matthew, Mark, Luke, and John rather than one work entitled "*The* Gospel.") Moreover, Paul's letters address a rather limited set of circumstances. It seems unfair to denounce him for not anticipating and addressing concerns that have only recently been raised to a high level of consciousness. This is *not* to say, however, that we can appeal to Paul's apparent acceptance of discrimination in his day to justify discrimination in our own. It is the gospel which Paul preaches rather than his limited application and witness to it that is definitive for our time. And that gospel has far-reaching implications for the full and equal realization of all human life.

We have sketched only broad contours in the history of interpretation of Paul. Hundreds of variations could be written on the five positions outlined here. Someone is bound to ask, "Is Paul worth all this attention?" Millions of hours of devoted labor have gone into the copying, translation, study, and interpretation of his letters. Tons and tons of paper and thousands of barrels of ink have gone into books and articles about him and his writings. Vast material resources have gone into great church buildings which bear his name, and the influence he exerted on key individuals like Augustine, Luther, Wesley, and others have had enormous historical consequences. One can easily imagine that Paul would be embarrassed by all this attention, and surprised if not horrified that his personal letters were canonized as Scripture. And yet the labors on his letters and the place they assume in the New Testament seem wholly justified. For he raised hard questions which the church had to face. And he dealt with real issues most of which still lie near the heart of humankind. Does history have a purpose? Can a broken and alienated world be reconciled? What is the nature of man? Can the whole human and nonhuman world be saved from its futility and grief? How can one live with partialities—partial sight, partial knowing, and partial being? And what does it mean to be alive "in Christ" and have Christ alive in oneself in an age of disbelief?

Notes

INTRODUCTION: CONTRARY IMPRESSIONS

1. *My Brother Paul* (New York: Harper & Row, Publishers, 1972), pp. 6ff.

CHAPTER 1. PAUL AND HIS WORLD

1. *Der Stil der paulinischen Predigt und die kynisch-stoische Diatribe* (Göttingen: Vandenhoeck and Ruprecht, 1910).
2. Victor C. Pfitzner, *Paul and the Agon Motif: Traditional Athletic Imagery in the Pauline Literature* (New York: Humanities Press, 1967).
3. Otto Michel, *Paulus und seine Bibel* (Gütersloh: C. Bertelsmann, 1929), p. 55.
4. Ernst Käsemann, *Perspectives on Paul*, trans. Margaret Kohl (Philadelphia: Fortress Press, 1971), pp. 104ff.; Rudolf Bultmann, *Theology of the New Testament*, trans. Kendrick Grobel (New York: Charles Scribner's Sons, 1951), II, 333, 140.
5. *Chapters in a Life of Paul* (Nashville: Abingdon Press, 1950), ch. 2.
6. Joachim Jeremias, "Paulus als Hillelit" in *Neotestamentica et Semitica: Studies in Honour of Principal Matthew Black,* ed. Edward Earle Ellis and Max Wilcox (Edinburgh: T. and T. Clark, 1969), pp. 88–94. Cf. also the classic work of Joseph Bonsirven, *Exégèse Rabbinique et Exégèse Paulienne* (Paris: Beauchesne and Sons, 1939).
7. Hans Joachim Schoeps, *Paul: The Theology of the Apostle in the Light of Jewish Religious History*, trans. Harold Knight (Philadelphia: The Westminster Press, 1961), p. 38.
8. Our word *eschatology* comes from two Greek words (*eschaton* and *logos*) which when taken together mean literally "thought about the end." The word as it is used by Biblical critics has come to denote God's decisive or final act in history. Apocalyptic literature is a highly imaginative literary account of God's revelation. In fact the word *apocalyptic* comes from the Greek word *apokalupsis,* which means revelation. Usually apocalyptic is more explosive than other eschatological pronouncements. Jesus' proclamation that the kingdom of God is at hand is eschatological. The vision of the beasts, fire, and astral pyrotechnics in the book of Revelation is apocalypticism. At the risk of oversimplification, we could say that all apocalyptic literature is eschatological (dealing with the end), but not all eschatological materials are apocalyptic. The term, eschatology, therefore, is the more general term. For a good discussion of apocalypticism see the *Interpreter's Dictionary of the Bible* (Nashville: Abingdon Press, 1962), I, 157–161.
9. Johannes Munck, *Paul and the Salvation of Mankind,* trans. Frank Clarke (Richmond: John Knox Press, 1959). For an excellent survey of the shifting sands of fate that apocalyptic has enjoyed (or suffered) in Pauline studies, see Klaus Koch's *The Rediscovery of Apocalyptic* (London: SCM Press, 1970).
10. Victor Tcherikover, *Hellenistic Civilization and the Jews,* trans. S. Applebaum (New York: Atheneum, 1970), pp. 349ff. and 303ff.
11. Erwin R. Goodenough, *Jewish Symbols in the Greco-Roman Period* (New York: Pantheon Books, 1953), I, 61ff.
12. W. D. Davies, "Paul and the Dead Sea Scrolls: Flesh and Spirit" in *The Scrolls and the New Testament,* ed. Krister Stendahl (New York: Harper and Brothers, 1957), p. 157.

13. *Judentum und Hellenismus* (Tübingen: J. C. B. Mohr [Paul Siebeck], 1969), esp. pp. 458–463. English translation: *Judaism and Hellenism* (Philadelphia: Fortress Press, 1974).

14. On this point Willem C. van Unnik is swimming against the stream when he juxtaposes Tarsus, "a typically Hellenistic city . . . the intellectual centre of a flourishing Stoic School," and Jerusalem, in which "syncretism secured no footing . . . and Hellenistic culture could force a way in only with difficulty and only very superficially." From *Tarsus or Jerusalem: The City of Paul's Youth* (London: Epworth Press, 1962), pp. 3–4. Van Unnik then argues that although Paul was born in Tarsus he was reared in Jerusalem where he received rabbinic training (p. 52).

15. Munck, *Paul and the Salvation of Mankind,* pp. 11–35.

16. If Paul has a favorite prophet it would appear to be Isaiah, whom he cites or alludes to more than twice as often as to Jeremiah. See the discussion in my *Judgement in the Community* (Leiden: E. J. Brill, 1972), pp. 153ff.

17. See especially Knox, *Chapters in a Life of Paul,* and more recently John C. Hurd, Jr., *The Origin of I Corinthians* (New York: Seabury Press, 1965).

18. 1 and 2 Corinthians, Philippians, and 1 Thessalonians. Galatians probably should be included, and the church in Rome likewise remained under the cultural influence of Hellenism. The fact that most of Paul's converts were poor does not isolate them from the spiritual and intellectual currents of the day. See Martin P. Nilsson, *Greek Popular Religion* (New York: Columbia University Press, 1940), reissued as *Greek Folk Religion* (New York: Harper Torchbooks, 1961).

19. Here I am following Munck, *Paul and the Salvation of Mankind,* pp. 36ff., and 303ff.

20. Nilsson, *Greek Piety* (Oxford: Clarendon Press, 1948), p. 188.

21. *Five Stages of Greek Religion* (Garden City, N.Y.: Doubleday & Co., 1955), p. 4.

22. See *Ancient Roman Religion,* ed. Frederick C. Grant (New York: Bobbs-Merrill Co., 1957), p. xxiv. For materials ascribed to the mysteries see *The New Testament Background: Selected Documents,* ed. Charles K. Barrett (New York: The Macmillan Co., 1957), pp. 92–104.

23. Bultmann, *Primitive Christianity in its Contemporary Setting,* trans. R. H. Fuller (New York: World Publishing Co., 1947), p. 159.

24. Ibid.

25. Ibid., p. 144.

26. The diatribe is a technique of argumentation. The speaker hears a hypothetical adversary raise objections which he then refutes. In Romans 4:1–2 and 6:1ff., objections to Paul's gospel are raised by a hypothetical objector. The objector, not the objections, is imaginary. Paul no doubt faced these questions many times.

27. Pythagoras lived and taught in the sixth century B.C. Epicureanism and the Imperial cult are not discussed here because their influence on Paul's hearers was minimal.

28. This is not to dispute the views of Tarn and Dodds that astrology came from the East. Not its origin but its manifestation in Greece is what concerns us here.

29. F. E. Peters, *The Harvest of Hellenism* (New York: Simon and Schuster, 1971), p. 431; H. J. Leon, *The Jews of Ancient Rome* (Philadelphia: Jewish Publication Society of America, 1961), pp. 243–257, 350–356; Tcherikover, *Hellenistic Civilization and the Jews,* pp. 301–308.

30. *Natural History*, trans. Harris Rackham, Loeb Classical Library (Cambridge, Mass.: Harvard University Press, 1938), II, v, 22.

31. Philostratus, *The Life of Apollonius of Tyana*, trans. F. C. Conybeare, Loeb Classical Library (Cambridge, Mass.: Harvard University Press, 1960); E. R. Dodds, *The Greeks and the Irrational* (Boston: Beacon Press, 1951), pp. 135–146, shows how interest grew in the philosophers as workers of miracles. David L. Tiede, *The Charismatic Figure as Miracle Worker* (Missoula, Mont.: Society of Biblical Literature, 1972), pp. 16ff., sees real tension between the traditions which view Pythagoras as a divine philosopher and those which remember him as a miracle worker. Tiede is right, of course, but it appears that the miracle-worker view was predominant in the first century.

32. *Life of Apollonius*, II, 315 (Bk. VIII, ch. vii).

33. See Holger Thesleff, *An Introduction to the Pythagorean Writings of the Hellenistic Period* (Abo: Abo Akademi, 1961).

34. Salo W. Baron, *A Social and Religious History of the Jews* (New York: Columbia University Press, 1952), I, 171.

35. Juvenal in his Satires XIV, as cited by Baron, *History of the Jews*, I, 179.

36. Ibid., p. 173.

37. Ibid., p. 171.

38. *The Life of Moses* (II, 27), trans. R. H. Colson, Loeb Classical Library (Cambridge, Mass.: Harvard University Press, 1959), VI, 463.

39. *Sympatheia* stands behind our word *sympathy*, meaning to suffer with someone. Here the word means to feel with or acknowledge kinship or relationship to all things so that what affects one part affects all of creation.

CHAPTER 2. THE ANATOMY OF THE LETTERS

1. For an up-to-date summary of the discussion so far, see William Doty, *Letters in Primitive Christianity* (Philadelphia: Fortress Press, 1973).

2. B. G. U. 27 (H. E. 113) as cited by Charles K. Barrett, *New Testament Background: Selected Documents* (New York: The Macmillan Co., 1957), p. 29.

3. Since there had been no attempt at this time to define life in Christ in terms of a system of belief, I realize the inappropriateness of this term. I use it, nevertheless, to show that some distinctions were being made between "true" and "false" apostles, prophets, etc. Paul himself rejected certain rival teachings as false.

4. (Berlin: Alfred Töpelmann, 1939).

5. See Erich Fascher, "Briefliteratur, urchristliche, *formgeschichtlich*" in *Die Religion in Geschichte und Gegenwart* (Tübingen: J. C. B. Mohr [Paul Siebeck], 3d ed. 1957), I, cols. 1412–1416.

6. The situation in 2 Corinthians is complicated by the likelihood that it is a composite of two or more letters. For a good discussion of the various possibilities see the English summary of Günther Bornkamm's "Die Vorgeschichte des sogenannten Zweiten Korintherbriefs" in *New Testament Studies*, 8 (1962), pp. 258–264.

7. See Fascher, "Briefliteratur," I, col. 1413.

8. "The Historicality of Biblical Language" in *The Old Testament and Christian Faith*, ed. Bernhard W. Anderson (New York: Harper & Row, 1963), pp. 132–149.

9. Robert W. Funk, *Language, Hermeneutic, and Word of God* (New York:

Harper & Row, Publishers, 1966), p. 270. He thinks Galatians and Romans are exceptions to this rule for good and sufficient reasons.

10. *Language*, p. 268. Funk also believes that the location of the announcement of his travel plans at the end of the letter is explicable in terms of Paul's imminent visit to Rome and the purpose the letter serves in preparing for that visit.

11. *Language*, p. 249.

12. Martin Dibelius, *Der Brief des Jakobus* (Göttingen: Vandenhoeck and Ruprecht, 11th ed. 1964), pp. 15ff.

13. For Hellenistic influence see Francis W. Beare, "The Epistle to the Colossians, Introduction" in *The Interpreter's Bible,* ed. George A. Buttrick et al. (Nashville: Abingdon Press, 1955), XI, 133ff. For Jewish and Hellenistic background see Siegfried Wibbing, *Die Tugend- und Lasterkataloge im Neuen Testament* (Berlin: Alfred Töpelmann, 1959).

14. David G. Bradley, "The *Topos* as a Form in the Pauline Paraenesis," *Journal of Biblical Literature,* 72 (1953), pp. 238–246.

15. Gordon Wiles, *Paul's Intercessory Prayers* (Cambridge: The University Press, 1973); William Doty, *Letters in Primitive Christianity;* and my own "1 Thessalonians 5:12–28: A Case Study," *Proceedings of the Society of Biblical Literature,* 108 (1972), II, 367–383. See Harry Y. Gamble, *The Textual History of the Letter to the Romans* (Claremont, Calif.: Paideia Press, forthcoming).

16. *The Oxyrhynchus Papyri,* ed. Bernard Grenfell and Arthur Hunt (London: Oxford University Press, 1910), III, 261–262.

17. Heikki Koskenniemi, *Studien zur Idee und Phraseologie des griechischen Briefes bis 400 nach Christus* (Helsinki: Akateeminen Kirjakauppa, 1956), pp. 169–180.

18. See my *Judgement in the Community* (Leiden: E. J. Brill, 1972), pp. 145, 161.

19. Even in the letter to Philemon Paul addresses "the church in your house" (vs. 2).

20. Victor Paul Furnish, *Theology and Ethics in Paul* (Nashville: Abingdon Press, 1968), p. 55.

21. See my *Judgement in the Community,* pp. 145ff., 161.

22. Paul sometimes dictates his letters to a secretary (amanuensis), appending a conclusion in his own hand. For instance, in Gal. 6:11ff., after he summarizes the central argument of the letter, he adds the conclusion with his "own hand." 1 Cor. 16:21–24 likewise displays an autograph. Although the secretary identifies himself in Rom. 16:22, doubt persists whether chapter 16 was part of the original letter (see ch. 4 below). On the strength of these two (or three) references it seems arbitrary to conclude that Paul dictated *all* his letters.

CHAPTER 3.   TRADITIONS BEHIND THE LETTERS

1. *The Apostolic Preaching and Its Developments* (London: Hodder & Stoughton, 1936), pp. 21–23.

2. "Even death on a cross" was probably inserted here by Paul.

3. My translation follows Ernst Lohmeyer's arrangement in his *Der Brief an die Philipper* (Göttingen: Vandenhoeck and Ruprecht, 19th ed. 1954), pp. 96ff.

4. The Greek *may* suggest an unreal past condition, "even *if* I had known him

(which of course I didn't) . . . ." Since we cannot be sure such was Paul's intention the following discussion is necessary.

5. Victor Paul Furnish, *Theology and Ethics in Paul* (Nashville: Abingdon Press, 1968), p. 55.
6. Joseph F. Fitzmyer, *Pauline Theology: A Brief Sketch* (Englewood Cliffs, N.J.: Prentice-Hall, Inc., 1967), p. 13.
7. Lloyd Gaston's *No Stone on Another* (Leiden: E. J. Brill, 1970), pp. 407–408, makes a good case for the authenticity of this saying.
8. *A Fresh Approach to the New Testament and Early Christian Literature* (New York: Charles Scribner's Sons, 1936), p. 143.
9. As Dibelius correctly notes in *A Fresh Approach*, pp. 143ff. William D. Davies, *Paul and Rabbinic Judaism* (London: S. P. C. K., 1948), p. 136, and Archibald M. Hunter, *Paul and His Predecessors* (London: SCM Press, 1961), pp. 52ff., go along.
10. Robert W. Funk, *Language, Hermeneutic, and Word of God* (New York: Harper & Row, Publishers, 1966), p. 270, and Furnish, *Theology and Ethics in Paul,* pp. 69ff., have forced a qualification of this earlier view.
11. Above, pp. 21–22.
12. *Theology and Ethics in Paul,* pp. 84–85.
13. David G. Bradley, "The *Topos* as a Form in the Pauline Paraenesis," *Journal of Biblical Literature,* 72 (1953), p. 246.
14. Of course those who argue for the authenticity of Colossians and Ephesians would add another category—rules for domestic life (*Haustafeln*). For example, see Col. 3:18–22: "Wives be subject to your husbands, as is fitting in the Lord. Husbands, love your wives, and do not be harsh with them. Children, obey your parents in everything, for this pleases the Lord. Fathers, do not provoke your children, lest they become discouraged. Slaves, obey in everything those who are your earthly masters." (See also Eph. 5:21–6:9.) Such instruction is unparalleled in the undisputed Pauline letters.

CHAPTER 4. THE LETTERS AS CONVERSATIONS

1. The 82-page book of Joseph F. Fitzmyer, *Pauline Theology: A Brief Sketch* (Englewood Cliffs, N.J.: Prentice-Hall, Inc., 1967), is excellent. Rudolf Bultmann's *Theology of the New Testament,* trans. Kendrick Grobel (New York: Charles Scribner's Sons, 1951), vol. I, is now almost a classic. Victor Paul Furnish, *Theology and Ethics in Paul* (Nashville: Abingdon Press, 1968), gives a good treatment of the major currents of Pauline interpretation.
2. The Greek word *ataktoi* refers not just to the idle, as is often assumed, but to those who create disorder. See 1 Cor. 14:40.
3. If the Thessalonians sent a letter to Paul with Timothy it probably contained requests for guidance on three items: (1) Paul had taught the members of the church to love the brethren. But it became a hot question whether one could love those who, expecting the end, had stopped work. Does love require that some be free at the expense of others? (2) Some members of the congregation had died. They were sincere when they accepted the gospel; they seemed to be as strong in their faith as anyone else. Does their death mean they were judged unworthy to enter the kingdom of God? If they were judged unworthy, how will anyone be saved? (3) Paul had taught that the end was near and the church had tried to prepare for it, but the end had not come. When would the end come?

Elsewhere (1 Cor.) Paul uses the phrase "now, concerning" to identify topics one by one that the churches had asked guidance on. A similar phrase appears in 1 Thess. 4:9 and 4:13, and a variation of the phrase appears in 5:1, leading some scholars to conclude that indeed the Thessalonians did write Paul a letter.

4. Some see 2 Cor. 6:14–7:1 as a fragment of the missing letter since it clearly is an insertion and since it deals with immorality—which Paul himself writes was the theme of his first letter (1 Cor. 5:9). Joseph A. Fitzmyer, however, has argued convincingly that the language is more characteristic of Qumran than of Paul; see his "Qumran and the Interpolated Paragraph in 2 Corinthians 6:14–7:1," *Catholic Biblical Quarterly*, 23 (1961), pp. 271ff.

5. In the discussion which follows I am greatly indebted to John C. Hurd, Jr., *The Origin of I Corinthians* (New York: Seabury Press, 1965).

6. Note especially Luke 20:34–36 which seems to suggest the same view: "And Jesus said to them, 'The sons of this age marry and are given in marriage; but those who are accounted worthy to attain to that age and to the resurrection from the dead neither marry nor are given in marriage, for they cannot die any more, because they are equal to angels and are sons of God, being sons of the resurrection'."

7. Because of the abrupt appearance of a new topic in the text, and because the command that women keep silent in church contradicts Paul's understanding of their role in 1 Cor. 11:5, it is widely assumed that 1 Cor. 14:33b–36 was inserted by a later hand to make the Corinthian letter conform to the viewpoint of the Pastoral epistles, especially 1 Tim. 2:11, "Let a woman learn in silence . . . ."

8. If 2 Cor. 10–13 originally belonged with chapters 1–9, then it was probably dictated a few days later. Notice the sharp change in tone between the end of chapter 9 and chapters 10–13. Bornkamm sees further divisions in chapters 1–9. For our purposes, however, whether chapters 1–9 (minus 6:14–7:1) were written at the same or different times is unimportant. The period of time over which 1–9 were written was so short that the practical result is a unified composition.

9. Scholars disagree on the location of these churches. According to the Southern Galatian theory they were in the region through which Paul traveled on his first missionary journey (Acts 13 and 14). This theory has the advantage of harmonizing Paul's letters with the Acts account. Those holding the Northern Galatian theory point to other discrepancies between Acts and Paul's letters and argue further that Paul uses the ethnic name "Galatians" (3:1) to refer to his readers, which would better befit the inhabitants of the north where the Galatians had settled than residents in the southern part of the Roman province of Galatia. Those opting for the Southern theory tend to date Galatians among the earliest of Paul's epistles since it is assumed that he founded the church on the first journey. Those supporting the Northern theory date Galatians later since it is assumed that it was on a later journey than the one described in Acts 13 and 14 that Paul penetrated to the heart of the old Celtic kingdom of Galatia (near modern Ankara, Turkey). The dating would also be of some significance if one were interested in trying to trace development in Paul's thought.

10. *Paul and the Salvation of Mankind*, trans. Frank Clarke (Richmond: John Knox Press, 1959), pp. 87–134.

11. In a paper, "Paul and Judaism with Illustrations from Galatians," delivered at the Annual Meeting of the Society of Biblical Literature, spring 1973.

12. Ingatius, *Epistle to the Philadelphians*, trans. Kirsopp Lake, Loeb Classical Library (Cambridge, Mass.: Harvard University Press, 1949), I, 245.
13. Gaston, "Paul and Judaism," p. 9.
14. I am indebted to Professor Nils Dahl for this insight which he put forth in a paper for the Paul seminar of the Society of Biblical Literature at the 1973 annual meeting. The paper, entitled "Paul's Letter to the Galatians: Epistolary Genre, Content, and Structure," will no doubt appear as part of a larger work on Galatians.
15. For the best defense of the hypothesis that Romans 16 was a part of Paul's original letter to the Roman church, see Harry Y. Gamble's *The Textual History of the Letter to the Romans* (Claremont, Calif.: Paideia Press, forthcoming).
16. (London: Faber and Faber, 1958), p. 116.
17. Victor Paul Furnish, *Theology and Ethics in Paul*, has shown that the ethical instruction in Paul's letters is not restricted to the closing sections.
18. Arguments for authorship in Rome: Paul mentions the "praetorian guard," "those of Caesar's household" and expects that the verdict will come soon. He realizes he may be executed.

    Against authorship in Rome: Members of the "praetorian guard" were present in most large population centers in the Empire. Likewise, "servants of the Emperor" (public as well as private) were to be found in other Mediterranean cities. Paul in this letter hopes to visit Philippi soon, which would take him back east from Rome. But we know from Romans that Paul fervently hoped to go from Rome to Spain (west). Finally, five communications between Paul and the Philippian church are assumed in the letter (the Philippians hear that Paul is jailed; they send Epaphroditus and hear later that he is sick; they communicate their concern to Paul, and he, in turn, communicates via letter with them). It would have taken approximately eight weeks to travel the distance between Rome and Philippi (nearly 800 miles). Would Paul be able to speak of "coming soon" if his prospective visit to Philippi were at the least months away? Although Ephesus is the leading rival to Rome as the place of Paul's imprisonment, a major objection to it is that Paul nowhere speaks of an Ephesian imprisonment.
19. Philippians is so loosely structured that many have suggested it is a patchwork of at least three fragments. Helmut Köster, "The Purpose of the Polemic of a Pauline Fragment (Philippians iii)," *New Testament Studies*, 8 (1962), p. 317, n.1, has a good survey of the literature on the subject. Even if we do have fragments from several letters, however, the essential elements in the conversation would remain, even if the order were altered somewhat.
20. See Walter Schmithals, "Die Irrlehrer des Philipperbriefs," *Zeitschrift für Theologie und Kirche*, 54 (1957), pp. 297ff.

CHAPTER 5. PAUL AND HIS MYTHS

1. This is Søren Kierkegaard's phrase, from *Philosophical Fragments*, trans. David F. Swenson (Princeton: Princeton University Press, 1962), pp. 68ff.
2. Henri Frankfort, *Before Philosophy* (Baltimore: Penguin Books, 1963), p. 16.
3. *Religion in Essence and Manifestation*, trans. J. E. Turner (New York: The Macmillan Co., 1938), p. 413.
4. *The Haggadah of Passover*, trans. Cecil Roth (London: Soncino Press, 1934), pp. 11–12 (emphasis added).

5. *The Way of Torah: An Introduction to Judaism* (Belmont, Calif.: Dickenson Publishing Co., 1970), p. 17. These ideas Neusner develops at much greater length; see especially his first chapter.
6. Mircea Eliade, *The Myth of the Eternal Return,* trans. Willard R. Trask (New York: Pantheon Books, 1954), p. 21.
7. "The Pauline Doctrine of the Lord's Supper" in *Essays on New Testament Themes* (London: SCM Press, 1964), p. 124.
8. *My Brother Paul* (New York: Harper & Row, Publishers, 1972), p. 173.
9. *The Last Adam* (Philadelphia: Fortress Press, 1966), p. 84.
10. *The Meaning of Revelation* (New York: The Macmillan Co., 1941), pp. 71–72.

CHAPTER 6. CURRENTS AND CROSSCURRENTS

1. Edgar Hennecke, *New Testament Apocrypha,* ed. Wilhelm Schneemelcher (Philadelphia: The Westminster Press, 1964), II, 122.
2. This unfortunate juxtaposition of Paul and Jesus is discussed below.
3. Since there was no sharp line between orthodoxy and heresy at this time, I realize a certain inappropriateness in using this term. I use it, nevertheless, for the sake of convenience.
4. *The Gospel of Philip,* trans. R. McL. Wilson (New York: Harper & Row, Publishers, 1966), p. 85.
5. From a "Life of Rabbula" composed by a colleague of the bishop and cited in Walter Bauer, *Orthodoxy and Heresy in Earliest Christianity,* ed. Robert A. Kraft and Gerhard Krodel (Philadelphia: Fortress Press, 2d ed. 1971), pp. 26–27.
6. Church leaders of both east and west whose writings were the chief sources of the emerging doctrine and observances of the church.
7. Origen, *Contra Celsum,* trans. Henry Chadwick (Cambridge: The University Press, 1965), Book III, chapter 42; Book IV, chapter 66.
8. See Maurice F. Wiles, *The Divine Apostle* (Cambridge: The University Press, 1967), p. 39.
9. See all six in Wiles, *The Divine Apostle,* p. 50.
10. Alexander Souter, *Pelagius's Expositions of Thirteen Epistles of St. Paul* (Cambridge: The University Press, 1926), vol. II, gives 120 pages of Latin text for the Romans commentary and 177 pages of commentary on the Corinthian letters.
11. J. N. D. Kelly, *Early Christian Doctrines* (London: Adam and Charles Black, 1958), p. 357.
12. Souter, *Pelagius's Expositions,* II, 45.
13. As cited in Jaroslav Pelikan, *The Christian Tradition, A History of the Development of Doctrine* (Chicago: University of Chicago Press, 1971), I, 315.
14. From *The Confessions,* Book X, chapter 29.
15. Heiko A. Oberman, *Forerunners of the Reformation* (New York: Holt, Rinehart and Winston, 1966), p. 126.
16. Oberman, *Forerunners,* p. 127.
17. William Wrede, "Paulus" in *Das Paulusbild in der neueren deutschen Forschung,* ed. Karl Heinrich Rengstorf (Darmstadt: Wissenschaftliche Buchgesellschaft, 1964), p. 94.
18. For a good critical assessment of Schweitzer's work on Jesus see James M. Robinson's Introduction to the 1968 edition of Schweitzer's *The Quest of the Historical Jesus* (New York: The Macmillan Co., 1968), pp. xi–xxxiii.

William D. Davies, *Paul and Rabbinic Judaism* (New York: Harper & Row, Publishers, 1967), pp. vii–xv, has an incisive statement on Schweitzer's estimation of Paul.

19. *The Confessions,* Book VIII, chapter 12, section 29.
20. André Dupont-Sommer, *The Essene Writings from Qumran,* trans. Géza Vermès (Cleveland: World Publishing Co., 1962), p. 102.
21. See his *Theology of the New Testament,* trans. Kendrick Grobel (New York: Charles Scribner's Sons, 1951), I, 190–352.
22. *Theology,* I, 285.
23. See the review of his book by William D. Davies in *New Testament Studies,* 2 (1955), pp. 60–72.
24. By restricting my comments to Munck's work I do not mean to slight the work of such eminent scholars as Ernst Käsemann, Krister Stendahl, C. Müller, P. Stuhlmacher, Davies, and others who differ from Bultmann. Munck was chosen here mainly to pose a sharp alternative to Bultmann's position.
25. "The Monstrous Imposition upon Jesus" in *The Writings of St. Paul,* ed. Wayne A. Meeks (New York: W. W. Norton & Co., 1972), p. 299.
26. Ibid.
27. "Paul: Chauvinist or Liberationist?" *The Christian Century,* 89 (1972), pp. 307–309; "Paul and the Eschatological Woman," *Journal of the American Academy of Religion,* 40 (1972), pp. 283–303; and most recently "Paul and the Eschatological Woman: Revisited," *Journal of the American Academy of Religion,* 42 (1974), pp. 532–537.
28. See especially Charles K. Barrett, *The First Epistle to the Corinthians* (New York: Harper & Row, Publishers, 1968), pp. 330–332.
29. See the relevant discussion above in chapter 4, "The Letters as Conversations."
30. "Paul and the Eschatological Woman: Revisited," p. 533.
31. Ibid. See Phil. 4:2–3 (Euodia and Syntyche who have "labored side by side with me in the gospel") and Rom. 16 if genuine. See 1 Cor. 16:19, which is certainly Paul's.
32. "Paul and Women: A Response to Recent Discussion," *Journal of the American Academy of Religion,* 42 (1974), pp. 538–549.
33. S. Scott Bartchy, *First-Century Slavery and 1 Corinthians 7:21* (Missoula, Mont.: Society of Biblical Literature, 1973), pp. 161–172, makes a strong case for this view.
34. Pagels, "Paul and Women," p. 545.
35. "Paul and Women," p. 544.
36. "Paul and Women," p. 544.
37. David Daube, "Pauline Contributions to a Pluralistic Culture: Re-creation and Beyond" in *Jesus and Man's Hope,* ed. Donald G. Miller and Dikran Y. Hadidian (Pittsburgh: Pittsburgh Theological Seminary, 1971), pp. 223–245.

Index